Cancer

*The Ultimate Guide to an Amazing Zodiac
Sign in Astrology*

Your Free Gift (only available for a limited time)

Thanks for getting this book! If you want to learn more about various spirituality topics, then join Mari Silva's community and get a free guided meditation MP3 for awakening your third eye. This guided meditation mp3 is designed to open and strengthen ones third eye so you can experience a higher state of consciousness. Simply visit the link below the image to get started.

https://spiritualityspot.com/meditation

Contents

Introduction

Perhaps you've had an interest in astrology for years, or maybe even decades, but you've never stretched past the generic information in newspapers and online. This ultimate guide walks you through every season and major element in a Cancerian life. Prepare to learn about your sign or the sign of someone you know and understand what it truly means to be a Cancer. You're not just born between June 21st and July 22nd; you're more than a crab that might be a bit sensitive. So many elements play into astrology, and the daily horoscope readings are just the cherry on top of a massive sundae.

The universe is in constant motion, and the ebb and flow of daily life feel a bit of that movement. When looking at astrology, there is a blend of science, belief, and phenomenon that has sparked rampant intrigue across the globe for centuries. Astrology is recovering quite a bit of its former craze, and people are beginning to question or wonder about the extent of the science behind something that seems fun and light-hearted. Astrology can tell you about your personality, emotional process, and even how you might interact with other people. This book is a great way to get an in-depth look into each element of being a Cancer or having a Cancer in your life. Use it as a chance to explore yourself, understand different facets of your personality, play to strengths, and overcome natural weaknesses.

Cancers are truly unique people who can face adversity, give sincere sympathy, and call up a strength within themselves that they may not have known to be there at all. Read on to find out more about the Cancer sign.

Chapter 1: A History of the Zodiac and Cancer, the Great Crab

We've lost endless volumes of knowledge through the ages, but one element of daily life that is making a resurgence is the Zodiac. Understanding the heavens, celestial bodies' movements, and the universe's impact on our lives each day is grabbing quite a bit of attention again. The Zodiac goes by many names. It is also known as the western Zodiac, as there is an Eastern Zodiac or the Chinese Zodiac. The twelve signs that make up the western Zodiac, also called houses, referring to both the sun and moon signs. These name fluctuations are relatively common knowledge, but they're the best place to start.

Throughout this text, you'll have the opportunity to learn about the fourth sign, Cancer. We'll refer to the western Zodiac as "the Zodiac" to keep things simple as we dive into the complex nuances of what it means to rule under the moon, how the term "cardinal" affects you or your loved ones, and what is so unique about this water sign.

To get started let's ease into the process by looking at the science and history behind the Zodiac. Astrology is still a science. It looks at the movements of celestial bodies, but it delves into the realm of theoretical and analyzes the impact on human affairs and the natural world. Fortunately, most of the research done on this was started thousands of years ago by a few of the best astrologers and astronomers from our world's ancient civilizations.

How the Zodiac Came to Be

At the beginning of the first millennium, Babylonian astronomers divided the heavens into the ecliptic Zodiacal signs. That sounds complex, but essentially, somewhere between 1,000 and 500 B.C., these astronomers began watching these twelve signs move across the sky in different positions through the seasons. After noticing their patterns, it was made into the Zodiac wheel well-known among people who follow astrology. This gave birth to astrology, but many of the stories and beliefs associated with these signs, and the constellations that are the Zodiac houses, stretch long before Babylon into Grecian and Egyptian studies and fables.

The earliest indicator of using the planets and stars to understand our world arose from those first Babylonian studies. In Ancient Babylon, the astronomers, who at the time were also in charge of astrology, would track the motions of Venus to identify planetary omens of bad times or good fortune to come. But we also know that the Egyptians employed planetary tracking, labeled constellations, and used planetary movements to make agricultural decisions. Babylon receives much of the claim to fame as Egyptians did not extensively document their tracking processes or respond to the movements. The major shift within the western Zodiac that delivered the system that we know and understand today took place in 330 B.C. when Alexander the Great conquered Egypt; Egyptian and Greek astronomers and people could then work together and exchange information they independently found about mathematics and logic. Together, they established strict rules such as the thirty-degree segmentation of the houses. They're also responsible for giving purpose to the Zodiac's circular structure which the Babylonians constructed. Eventually, they aligned their positions in the sky to the seasons and correlated the movements to other stars and planetary changes. At this point, ancient astronomers laid out the foundation of what we know of astrology's scientific and mathematical elements. Many significant developments have come, but the old traditions accumulated over thousands of years remain in place.

It's well worth noting that the Egyptian, Greek, and Babylonian cultures aren't solely responsible for the Zodiac. Hebrew practice, specifically the Hebrew Bible, aligns with many astrology points and is primarily the reason for a few of the most well-known characteristics of people born under specific Zodiac signs. Unlike the other cultures, the Zodiac's Hebrew elements looked explicitly at the quarter-landing signs or signs that directly affected the seasons changing, rather than looking at all twelve signs equally. The Hebrew contribution to the Zodiac mostly revolves around Leo, Taurus, Aquarius, and Scorpio. But just because these teachings don't have a hyper-focus on Cancer doesn't mean that their research, studies, stories, and culture don't impact the sign. Thomas Mann authored a novel called "Joseph and his Brothers" which looked at Israel's twelve tribes, assigning each to a specific characteristic associated with a singular Zodiac sign. The creatures representing Leo, Taurus, Aquarius, and Scorpio all appear as the quarter signs in the Book of Ezekiel. It acknowledges that these are the signs that align with the lunar year of the Zodiac. A bit later in this chapter, we'll evaluate these, and you'll see much more of this throughout the book as well.

As the Zodiac developed and appeared in more cultures worldwide, people began associating personality traits and characteristics with different Zodiac signs. This stretches as far back as Egyptian and Grecian times when they represented celestial figures that came with stories, fables, and even godly worship. The signs emblems, symbols, and roots that we know today came as a result of all of this rich history melding together over the years. One major moment that brought these observations and thousands of years of study together occurred in the 15th and 16th centuries. During the 15th century, astronomers began working with *volvelle*, or movable devices, to work out the sun and moon's positioning with respect to the Zodiac. During the 16th century, those mechanisms were used to give more foundation to each of the signs, and then 16th-century artists began cultivating pictorial representations with this new information.

Sun Signs and Moon Signs

As a quick overview, there are twelve Zodiac signs, also called Sun Signs. Because we know more about the sun's changing situation with the constellations and celestial bodies, Sun Signs are favored, but there are also the moon and rising signs.

The twelve signs of the western Zodiac include Aries, Taurus, Gemini, Cancer, Leo, Virgo, Libra, Scorpio, Sagittarius, Capricorn, Aquarius, and Pisces. Each name of the Zodiac ties to a direct constellation that matches up with the dates of when the sun is in that house. They gained popularity as a result of the astronomer Ptolemy, who tracked the movements of the constellations in conjunction with the sun's position, one of the reasons we refer to them as sun signs.

Cancers are born between June 21st and July 22nd when the sun is in the house of Cancer the Crab. This book is going to dive into exactly how Cancers work and how the world around them might impact them on different levels. Each person presents a unique representation of their sun sign. Still, they're also affected by their moon sign, Rising Sun Sign, and other astrological elements that go beyond the basics of their sun sign. As you read through this, we hope that you can gain a complete understanding of how changes in astrology and the founding principles impact your life or that of a Cancer that you know.

Moon signs are a bit different from sun signs, and they're far more difficult to calculate. With a sun sign, you simply have to know your birthdate, and then you know your Zodiac sign. But the moon signs change constantly; you must know your birth date and the hour of your birth. Sometimes even the difference of a single minute can change your moon sign. Your moon sign depends on calculating your full birth date and the place and time to calculate the moon's position at the moment of your birth. Many quick and easy online calculators do the complex work for you as long as you have the basic information.

So, what do moon signs do? A sun sign is taken as an indicator of personality, and essentially your charge or frequency within the universe. A moon sign plays less into your personality and more into your emotions and management of those emotions. Cancers are notoriously private, but also sensitive. That sensitivity can make them especially in-tune with their moon sign. For a quick example, and we'll have many of these throughout the book, someone born on June 30th of 1995 at nine in the evening in Los Angeles would have the moon sign of Leo. They would have all the personality traits of a Cancer but would process their emotions in a much more "Leo" way and may be more likely to step outside of their shell from time to time. With a Cancer-Leo combination, this person might feel less self-critical or may not care as much about what others think when compared to a Cancer-Cancer combination. But the traits of a moon sign differ slightly from the characteristics of the mirrored sun sign. Those with the moon sign of Cancer would be high attuned to other's emotions and would likely be highly sympathetic, a real-life empath.

The last of the Zodiac signs that deserves a fair amount of attention is the rising sign. This is a form of your sun sign correlating to your outward style or what you project to the world around you. If your sun sign is the energy or vibration that you have in connection with the universe, then the rising sun sign is the vibration or frequency you emit specifically when you're around others.

Calculating a rising sign also requires knowing your place and time of birth. The example we used above of the person born on June 30th would result in a Capricorn ascending sign. That means that Capricorn's sign was rising to the suns position at the time of this person's birth. Again, the rising sign depicts the more social version of their personality. In the example, the person might have a greater sense of outward accountability and responsibility. A person with a Cancer ascending sign might be shy or wary of new people and might seek outright isolation. Cancer-rising people are often inherent introverts or extremely low within the extraversion scale.

How Can Learning About A Sun Sign Impact You?

When science seems so certain, but the authority figures behind it seem unreliable, many people turn back to the tried-and-true astrology approach. A National Science Foundation poll from 2014 indicated that more than half of Millennials believe astrology to be a science.

The foundations of mathematics and logic which drive astrology play a bigger role than other less scientifically-founded astrology elements. But even though less scientific elements of astrology can offer a lot of insight into a person's personality, communication preferences, and daily approaches to life, it's a mixture of fun and science. Take a look at how celestial movements may have affected your birth, childhood, love life, career path, and many other life elements.

Having a spouse, friend, child, sibling, or even co-worker born under the Cancer sign can be quite a mystery. This is, without a doubt, one of the most intriguing signs in the Zodiac, and it offers an allure that draws people into the unknown. People born under the Cancer sign can be strong but sensitive and possessed of all other oxymoronic combinations. If you know someone was born under the

Cancer sign, then you've seen these opposing personality traits work together seamlessly to deliver an action-oriented, empathetic, and productive person.

When looking at the history of Cancer and the constellation representing that house, it's clear that there are many strong elements, underlying weaknesses, and essentially human traits. The constellation Cancer, which is Latin for "crab", lies in the northern sky. It is nestled between Leo and Gemini, has a 20° north declination, and has many star clusters but most notably the Beehive. The constellation story goes back to Greek mythology and is occasionally represented by a crawfish or a lobster. The story goes that this is the crab that pinched Heracles while he was fighting the Hydra.

After pinching Heracles, the crab was crushed. Hera, the goddess of women, marriage, and family, was an enemy of Heracles and rewarded the crab for its valiant efforts by placing the crab in the heavens.

For many people, the Zodiac is a bit of fun, but knowing your sign's roots, position, element, and other minute details can help you understand parts of your personality. Knowing in-depth information about Zodiac signs can help one be very insightful into the lives of people born under each sign. The Zodiac history, the heavens' movements, and the stories tied into the constellations are woven throughout the Zodiac and feature heavily in our lives. Is it any wonder that a sign celebrated by Hera represents a mothering nature? Throughout this book, you'll get an in-depth look at the different seasons that a Cancer will go through in life and how you, or your friend, can make the most of their natural strengths. Along with understanding and building upon those natural Cancer strengths, they can learn how to work around the possible downsides as well.

Being a Cancer, or knowing and loving one, is an extraordinary thing. Here you'll learn what Cancers are like on their own, a seldom-approached element of their life. You'll also have the opportunity to learn more about Cancers as children, the careers they thrive in, and how they are affected by the ever-changing presence of the heavens and the surrounding energy.

Chapter 2: Cancer Basics

Everything you need to know about the basics of Cancer in astrology is in this chapter. While much of this information is common knowledge, you'll have the opportunity to assess the information associated with these basic elements that are often glossed over online or even in most horoscope books. What does it mean to be a water sign? You might know you're a cardinal sign, but what is that, and how does it impact your life?

These are the questions we hope to discuss as we review the fundamentals of the Cancer sign within astrology and begin our deep dive into Cancerian lifestyles.

The Fundamentals of Cancer Life

Cancer is the sign of the great Crab, it's the fourth in the Zodiac Circle and is for those exclusively born between June 21st and July 22nd.

An overview of all Cancer fundamentals:

- Born between June 21st and July 22nd
- Ruled by the Moon
- Water element
- Cardinal

• Represents the Chest or Torso

Of course, many other fundamentals come with being a Cancer. It's likely that as Cancer, you have various positive traits associated with the sign, such as a great sense of loyalty, powerful intuition, and empathetic nature. You may also experience the natural drawbacks such as moodiness, pessimism, and being rather suspicious of those around you.

Cancer life always comes back to these core elements. The positive traits, weaknesses, and relationships all root in Cancer's element, ruling planet, quality, and even power colors or crystals.

What a Cardinal Position Means

Even those who follow their horoscope or the Zodiac often neglect their sign's position or quality element. Cancers are in a cardinal position or offer a cardinal quality, which is important not only to the sign's history but also to the two core elements of most Cancerian personalities.

Common personality elements of cardinal signs include:

• Ability to overcome challenges with ease

• Affinity and acumen at the hands-on approach

• Perceived as natural leaders

Within the Zodiac, there are four cardinal signs: Aries, Cancer, Libra, and Capricorn. These are identified as cardinal signs because they are reactive or important, because they mark the turning point of a season. The word itself, cardinal, stems from the Latin word for important, and these signs occur at key times that would have been highly important to ancient civilizations. Although we don't put much thought into changing seasons now, the beginning of the summer solstice stood as a pivotal moment in the year for almost every ancient civilization that contributed to astrology.

The summer solstice takes place on June 20th, with the house Cancer taking it over the following day. On ancient Greek calendars, it was evident that the summer solstice and entering the house of Cancer were important to the culture. The summer solstice began a one-month countdown to the Olympic Games, brought forth the Festival of Cronus, and during this time of change and celebration, the Greek social structure was completely ignored. Everyone from royalty to slaves participated in the celebrations openly. Pagan traditions for the summer solstice were midsummer, and even Native American tribes had solstice celebrations and traditions.

Being a cardinal sign and understanding the many celebrations that occurred at this time of year is important because it explains a lot of the Cancer personality. Cancerians are known to have a wishy-washy nature; they often change their minds, and their emotions tend to ebb and flow with greater variety than non-cardinal signs. Cancers may be wary of change when it's put into motion by others, but when they're in charge, the change is impactful, even though possibly temporary.

Within the four cardinal signs, there is further division. Cancer is seen as the emotional well or the heart of the cardinal signs. Cancer is already emotion-driven as a water sign, and as a cardinal water sign, Cancerians push the limits for feelings and communication.

The Cancer Element – Water

Having twelve houses, each of the astrological signs is attached to an element. Cancer, the crab sign, is attached to the water element. Typically, water signs are emotionally sensitive and generally self-protective, which ties into their sensitive nature. They must be certain of their emotional grounding and make decisions that don't make much sense to others because Cancerians are looking at every possible angle before deciding what to do.

Key traits of water signs:

- Extremely observant

- Intense emotional connection

- Often lost in thought (Cancers tend to get lost in the past)

- Crave inclusion

- Mysterious

- Creative and innovative thinkers

Often, water signs are led toward the arts and useful hobbies that can help others. But why water? Cancer, represented by the Crab, seems quite at home in the water. The earth is habitable because of water, and we engage with water every day through humidity, snow, steam, vapor, and of course, water in its liquid state.

Water signs can lack direction, feel listless, and be lost in decision making. Cancer's cardinal position makes it prime for water-signs advantages while mitigating many of the downsides. Other water signs like Scorpio may tend to lack direction, but Cancers' cardinal position pushes them with considerable momentum. Cancers may change and are indecisive at times, but there is no hesitation in decision-making and no sensation of listlessness when they choose to do something.

Water signs are also known for being in tune with their emotions. Again, their experiences with emotions depend on their position within the Zodiac. As a water element with a cardinal position, Cancers are subject to a lot of emotional change and receptiveness. To offer a comparison to another astrological sign, Pisces is also a water sign, but they're in the mutable. When it comes to the combination of water and the mutable position, Pisces tend to be emotionally static and, rather than receptive, assistive. So Pisces would, at a point, stop listening and rush off to do what they think is best, where Cancers tend to listen to the troubles and offer little advice but rather let the person in need take the lead.

Ruling Planet

Sure, the moon might not necessarily be a planet, but it is vital to the Cancer sign and has a pivotal contribution to astrology. Within astrology, the moon is recognized as the fastest moving element in the universe in terms of relative motion. As a fast-moving planet, the moon is known for its tendency toward change, and it greatly affects each person's unique star chart. Moon astrology is a vital element of overall astrology, and as we mentioned in chapter one, the moon isn't just a planet recognized in astrology. It also comes with an assigned moon sign.

The moon represents all things that we would find within ourselves, such as preferences, dislikes, fears, emotion, and the soul itself. As a sign ruled under the moon, Cancers are known for their peace-loving nature and their ability to understand emotion within themselves and within others.

If you're feeling disappointed with the moon as the ruling planet, we're going to dive directly into the high level of importance that the moon plays within astrology. First, the moon begins its starting point in Cancer, it starts in the fourth house, and it ends in Scorpio. That means that Cancer is the first moon sign, and Scorpio is the last. Second, the moon itself is more likely to experience interactions with asteroids or meteors, given that it lacks an atmosphere. This means that it is far apart from any other celestial entity, with its only close relation being the Sun.

Finally, the Sun and the Moon have more relationships in astrology than most people would imagine. We mentioned that there are Sun Signs and moon signs. We also mentioned that both the Sun and the moon lack an atmosphere; that differentiates them from any other celestial entity. Our final point in the moon's importance as a ruling planet and specifically as Cancer's ruling planet is that the Sun and the moon are not competitors.

The moon is an aide or an assistant to the Sun. Across the endless civilizations, there is a clear divide between light and dark. But it is the moon that brings light into the darkness of night. Many fables and beloved stories recognize that the moon and the Sun are closely tied because the moon itself reflects the light of the Sun and provides that light to disrupt darkness.

With the moon as Cancer's ruling planet, Cancerians are in a uniquely powerful position to disrupt darkness, forge new light, and provide swift change for inner elements of ourselves.

Various Houses

Cancer is within the House of Moods, the fourth house of the Zodiac, and the ruling planet being the moon further enhances that presence of emotions. That is further enhanced by their water element, which ties directly to feeling, and even further by their quality as a cardinal position tying them to change.

Not all signs have this grand buildup of a singular characteristic or core element for their personality. It's pretty rare, which makes Cancerians truly unique. They are within the House of Moods and Emotions, but their planet represents emotional awareness. Their position indicates times of change, and their element is that tied to emotional connection.

Cancers have another affinity, that for the house, family, and home. Cancers will often feel a deep attachment to home or a deep need to create a home of their own. They often surround themselves with the people that they hold dear, whether that's blood relation or otherwise, and create a home environment wherever they land.

Power Colors

Tying back to the moon itself, Cancer's power colors are silver, cream, gray, and white. Not only should you feel a surge of energy and positivity when wearing or donning these colors, but others around you should feel it, too.

Understand the meanings of these colors to get more aligned with your Cancer power colors. Silver largely represents grace and sophistication, while cream or beige represents calm and serenity. These two colors can do well in your living space, as well as your closet.

Cancer Personality Traits

With the Cancer sign, it is easy to see how each sign's element leads into the other. There is a strong overarching sense of emotion, change management, and introspective attention. Being a Cancer ruled under the moon as a cardinal quality and home to the fourth house produce many Cancer personality traits that clearly make sense.

Cancers are often emotional, which is no surprise. But a few of the most famous Cancerians have shown off their emotions in drastically different ways. Elon Musk is a Cancer. Although he works in the Sciences rather than the Arts, it's evident from his passionate speaking and presence that he's largely ruled by emotion. Few can forget the emotional impact evident on Elon Musk's face when his rocket was a success.

The 14th Dalai Lama and Nelson Mandela are both notable Cancerians showing the true depth and complexity of this sign's personality traits. Kind heartedness, love for others, and an emotional connection to others in the world are present in these two outstanding figures.

When exploring the importance of the ruling planet for Cancer being the moon, it was emphasized that the moon's rule is to shed light in the darkness. One of the most astounding traits in the Zodiac falls to Cancer, and it's their innate ability to spark happiness in others even when they themselves are not feeling great. There's a long list of Cancerian actors and entertainers who made careers out of this personality trait. Most notably perhaps is Robin Williams. Would anyone else have made such emotionally charged movies such as "Patch Adams", "What Dreams May Come", "Aladdin", "Jack", or the many others to which he lent his talents?

Other entertainers and comedians that have used their ability to bring happiness and dive deep into their emotions include Patrick Stewart, Dan Aykroyd, John Goodman, Kristen Bell, Nicole Kidman, and Meryl Streep.

Cancerians are often shy and typically need a lot of time alone. Still, they are pulled into the spotlight because of their tendency to be natural leaders and their inclination toward kindness and positivity. Combining these personality traits can turn people into natural leadership roles such as running a household, running a company, or helping people in their life without any official leadership title.

There is a special mention for those born within three days of June 21st or July 22nd, otherwise known as the cusp. While you are still a Cancer and everything you've read here still applies to you, it may be slightly muddled or altered depending on the cusp sign. Typically, those of the Gemini-Cancer cusp have an enhanced version of most of the Cancer personality traits and respond with greater enthusiasm to the Cancer sign's foundational elements. They are often more loyal and more likely to ebb and flow between moderate or extreme emotions. It's almost as if the spring to summer transition heightens the change and celebrational elements of the Cancer sign.

The Cancer-Leo cusp, which spans from July 19th to July 25th, is a different story. While these Cancerians are usually empathetic and in tune with themselves, they're offset by the purest fire sign. When the highly emotional Cancer and the ego-driven Leo meet, you get someone who's confident and empathetic but possibly to the point of being overzealous or even manipulative. Those born on the Cancer-Leo cusp might be more inclined to take active leadership positions, drive change, and insert themselves into causes they care about that require an assertive hand. It's a stark difference from the calm, kind, and sensitive Gemini-Cancer cusp.

It's the culmination of the very foundation of the Cancer sign which resulted in many Cancerian strengths. The personality traits listed here are not outright strengths, but they can lend themselves towards being a positive force or a negative element in a Cancer's life.

Chapter 3: Cancer Strengths

Motivated by deep emotional connection, recharging through intimate time spent alone, and developing family relationships within their inner circle are just a few ways of seeing Cancer people from an outward perspective. But much like a crab, all the good stuff is under the shell, and that outer appearance doesn't prepare anyone for what lies beneath. Cancers are well-known for their strengths and appreciated as many of the most compassionate and strong characters among the Zodiac. These individuals are often sought and kept as lifelong friends because of this combination of strengths.

If you were born under the fourth house, then these strengths may seem like natural parts of your personality. They may not even seem like strengths to you, as many of Cancerians' strengths also lend themselves to weaknesses. Almost all of these strengths are a double-edged sword, but that makes it even easier for a Cancer who understands themselves to play up their strengths often and in doing so lower, if not eliminate, many of the weaknesses they face as parts of their personality.

If you know a Cancer, then these strengths won't surprise you, and it's likely that you've experienced the benefits of many of these strengths frequently. Friends, spouses, and family members of Cancer people often love having them around because of the strengths they bring into everyday situations. Those who know Cancerians should be careful not to take advantage of these personality traits or extort them explicitly for their own benefit. Typically, Cancers aren't aware of their many abilities and what they bring to the table because they're so often concerned with the other people around them. When a Cancer person recognizes that they're only kept around for specific elements of their personality, they tend to recede and feel used. They don't stick around long when it seems like they aren't truly loved, but only appreciated for one part of themselves. Cancers want pure, unconditional love, not to be kept around for someone else's benefit. You'll see through their many strengths that Cancerians can benefit from their own strengths as much as anyone else can, and that they can set healthy boundaries to make sure they're not taken advantage of and that their interactions are mutually enjoyed.

Compassionate and Empathetic

Those born under the Cancer sign are among the most compassionate and empathetic people you'll ever meet. But compassion and empathy are two different strengths that Cancers have. They're combined here because of their similarities and their roots in emotions and feelings.

Compassion, or being compassionate, has a core in suffering and pity. The word "compassion" has a Latin root of *pati*, and that root word means "to suffer". Giving someone compassion means connecting with them in their suffering and relating to their pain. That relation and connection are like lending that person a bit of strength. Essentially, Cancers have the innate ability to say, "You're going through something rough, and I'm here for you. I understand you and know that you're so strong for getting through this." That is compassion. Cancers know that the other person doesn't always need them to jump into action, sometimes they just need to hear a sympathetic acknowledgment of what the sufferer is facing.

Female cancers are more likely to have higher levels of compassion. Male cancers do have compassion, but they may have higher expectations of the other person involved. Male and female Cancers have different nurturing ways, and often, female Cancers offer more sensitivity, whereas male Cancers offer a bit of a push in the right direction. Having compassion, showing condolence, and offering pity all come down to the heart and head sensitivity that Cancers experience as water signs. When it comes to the elements that make up the strength for a Cancerian, it's obvious that this is their most prominent strength no matter their gender, and it can even break down the barriers that cusp babies might feel. Those on the Gemini cusp might have more of this trait than those on the Leo cusp. Gemini, as an air sign, has a lot more in common with this water sign, whereas Leos, as a fire sign, often contradict the very strength that Cancers possess.

Empathy is a different matter; a strength for others, but often a drawback for an untrained Cancerian. Empathy is a skill that Cancers need to learn, even though it's a natural part of their personality. Cancers are natural empaths, but they don't naturally align with this skill from birth; it is something that they have to dedicate time toward developing.

The definition of empathy is the action of understanding and being aware of the feelings of others. This definition expands to include experiences, thoughts, feelings, and emotions of others, either past or present. When discussing empathy as an ability, we're talking about the inherent ability to take understanding those emotions, feelings, and thoughts to a deeper level. Empaths don't just understand; they experience the feelings, emotions, and thoughts as if they were happening to them directly. They feel it as raw and as openly as if they experienced the event or feeling first-hand. As children, these kids have huge feelings that any other sign as a parent may see as overwhelming or outright unmanageable. But Cancerians need to develop this skill as though it were a school subject, psychic ability, or athletic skill. They must engage in empathy practice and be receptive to their abilities as they develop and adapt. When properly prepared, a Cancer could be the go-to counselor in the family, workplace, or among friends. They are often the ones to solve problems and work through people-problems in small groups. Cancerians are aces at cognitive empathy, making them excellent with people even when they're introverted.

Because of these two abilities, Cancer should never lack genuine friends and should always understand complex or advanced emotions far beyond their years. They understand the effect on those who experienced an event first-hand but always offer the compassion to exercise their understanding in accepting the person's experience as unique to them.

These two abilities go back to two distinct elements in this Zodiac sign. First is the connection to the moon and the moon's representation of the soul, emotions, and all things "under the surface". Second is their root in the ocean, where emotions run deep and the desire to connect with others goes even deeper. Even those on the cusps will have powerful elements from these strengths in their daily lives, and these two strengths lend themselves toward a third: listening. These two elements come together to create excellent listeners. On a good day, the sympathetic and emphatic Cancerian can bolster others' confidence and strength, as well as their own. On a bad day, they can use these strengths to manipulate a situation in their favor or, inversely, become overrun with emotion and seclude themselves. But even when alone, or even when using their abilities for their own ends, it's not the worst results of these two strengths. Cancers aren't prone to manipulation and often use it as a last resort when they feel extremely vulnerable, so even at the end of a bad day, this is still a strength for the Cancer.

Ability to Find Happiness

Where many signs see happiness or despair, light or dark, the crab likes to scuttle sideways and walk the fine line between the two. Their ability to approach situations in unexpected and indirect ways often allows them to find happiness where it seems that there's nothing to be found but dissatisfaction.

When J. K. Rowling wrote the famous line, "Happiness can be found even in the darkest of places, if only one remembers to turn on the light," she may as well have been talking about Cancers specifically, and you'd better hope that you have a Cancer around in dark times. Without a doubt, they'll be the ones to find the light switch, strike the match, or pull back the veil to let the light in on the world.

That doesn't mean that Cancer's aren't plagued by bouts of darkness occasionally, but usually, they're at their most despondent when this happens. It's not common for Cancers to go through bouts of deep depression or experience chronic depression, but lower levels of discontentedness are likely seasonal. It isn't any shock when you learn that a Cancer experience Seasonal Anxiety Disorder or simple rounds of the Winter Blues.

Cancers are naturals when it comes to bringing happiness and contentment to the forefront. Suppose you notice that a particular Cancer, perhaps yourself, leans toward a pessimistic disposition. In that case, this could largely be attributed to your moon sign, as you may have congestion in managing your heightened sensitivity to emotions. That congestion or pessimism could be an effect of the self-preservative nature of Cancers. Cancers are more highly attuned to their moon sign than any other astrological sign, and their heart and head sensitivity to emotions often mean that their moon sign can dampen this strength if they don't know how to manage it properly. Understand a bit more about your moon sign and know that each astrological sign's moon-sign effects are different from the sun sign effects. For example, those born under the Cancer moon sign are less likely to accept change and are often deeply rooted in familiarity and security. They may be less likely to see the good in various opportunities or less inclined to look for a solution when they would rather sulk. This is quite different from the Cancer's sun sign inclining them to find light in the darkness. Explore your moon sign more to understand how you can use this strength to the best of your abilities.

This strength ties back to the cardinal element of the sun sign for Cancer. As a cardinal sign, they're leading the changes in life, knowing that there's always something positive or beneficial on the other side of that change. They tend to live in the realm of perceived abundance and often are happy with circumstances and material possessions far below their means.

A special note for Cancer-Leo cusps: this may be a struggle. Balancing the regal and somewhat materialistic Leo tendencies with this Cancer happiness should be easy, but you might occasionally feel torn.

Concerned About Fairness

Cancers are advocates for justice in the way that they see as most fair. They're often the ones to foster a compromise agreement between two or more people that are struggling to agree or work together. This strength comes from the house and element. Not only are Cancers attuned to the mysteries of the ocean, but also its naturally stable ecosystem. There are undercurrents, currents, and natural changes, and Cancerians feel all of that. In their mind, things should work a certain way, within reason. They're looking at compromise and what it would take to create win-win scenarios with little effort. But when it's evident that one person is outright unruly or unfair, then they step in with their claws.

Very Loyal

Their loyalty level is definitely a strength, but it does lead to the negative side-effect of leaving them averse to seeing unsavory elements of their friends or family. Their loyalty is above par, and they substantiate it with honesty, good listening, and genuine concern.

These are the people who prove their loyalty by listening and working with their friend, colleague, partner, or family member toward accepting or correcting any situation. To get their loyalty to such a high level, Cancerians often develop solid friendships very early in life and then cultivate new relationships with an air of caution because they know what they may have to put into a relationship.

This strength makes them exceptional friends and employees. They are great when they have a particular person to direct this loyalty towards, which often leads Cancerians into long-term relationships. Even though Cancers enjoy time alone, they often feel at their best when they're in a stable relationship, and they're usually the ones who bring that stability. A person in a relationship with a Cancer needn't have any trust issues, but they might struggle to keep the Cancer happy and match this level of loyalty. Cancers don't expect much more than standard loyalty; they don't expect people to match their loyalty level, although it often brings out the best in other signs as people feel the need to reciprocate what they've received from a Cancer. Cancer's loyalty isn't just a strength for others to benefit from; it often means that they have the best connection with their friends, spouse, and close family members. They can trust the people in their lives without a doubt because of this loyalty, and that loyalty brings out the best qualities in others.

When it comes to lost trust Cancers have different ways of responding to loyalty changes. For example, if faced with a cheating spouse, a woman Cancer might place loyalty over self-preservation. This is part of their personality, they love this person, and they're loyal because of that love so voiding that loyalty wouldn't just be a loss of that person in their life but the love they experience as well. It may be self-protective to stay and reap what they can from the relationship until the trust is so diminished that the loyalty has no foundation and crumbles.

A male Cancer, or a Leo-Cancer cusp (man or woman), would likely end the relationship immediately because their loyalty is more malleable than that of a female Cancerian. Even Gemini-Cancer cusp people may turn away from a relationship if they feel their loyalty was exploited or unappreciated.

Overall, a Cancer's loyalty is a strength because of what it brings into the Cancer's life, not because of what they give to others. They cultivate better friendships and can count on people more reliably than other signs because of their innate loyalty which tends to bring out the best in those around them.

Imaginative

Cancers see unexpected ways of approaching life, whether it's something fun and explorative or something technical. Cancers are many of your top problem-solvers for people issues, and they have a great capacity for creative imagination as well. This can seem like a Cancer is shutting down, because they're usually secluded or enjoying alone- time when they're utilizing their creative side. Cancers don't always want alone time to get away from people, although it might seem that way; they really just want the chance to explore and imagine without distraction.

Cancer men do best when they're left to their own devices and can think about everyday things like driving or shopping. They'll often come up with off-the-wall ideas, although they may not always follow up on them. Cancerian women usually need alone time or dedicated time to imagine and explore creative pursuits. They don't want someone intruding on their thoughts, and they don't want distractions pulling them away from their interests. Cancer-Leo cusps may be more prone to exploring their imaginative gifts in both communication and creative fields with other people around them. They may take on group projects or lead innovative ideas from start to finish.

Cancers typically prefer to work with little supervision and virtually no restrictions, as they don't want anyone putting a damper on their ability to work creatively and spend time imagining. This Cancerian strength lends itself to others in many ways. They often tend to attract others who are creative as well and foster deeply loyal connections with them. Cancerians may also use this strength to build up people going through a rough patch or find creative solutions to people's problems. Overall, these strengths make them one of the most precious signs within the Zodiac, as nearly all of these strengths benefit others as well as themselves. Cancerians aren't prone to an excessive ego, making them extremely selfless and caring. Their deep connection to the moon and the ocean, balanced with the cardinal-sign ability to adapt to change, means that they're constantly thinking about what they can do for those around them in a way that also allows them to protect themselves. It's astounding how one sign can bring so much happiness and clarity to the world.

Chapter 4: Cancer Weaknesses

Let's talk about weaknesses because we all have them, even the Leo's, who tend to believe they're the baddest lions in the universe. Those who are Cancer-Leo cusps may be all too familiar with this over-confident mindset, and the fact that they may even openly believe that they're outright unstoppable, invincible, or completely without fault. Everyone has faults, even Cancer-Leos, and of all the possible faults, Cancerians really have it pretty easy.

Across the board, their weaknesses are similar, except for Cancer-Leo cusps, who feel a few of these faults a little harder than the other Cancers. Often these weaknesses appear in flares or as spurts and then subside quickly. The drawback is that it seems Cancerians are prone to extreme mood swings and that they're inconsistent. That's true sometimes, but Cancers just can't help it. They feel big feelings, and when the mood strikes, they can be needy, too connected to the past, or prone to passive-aggressive outbursts. These usually surprise everyone else around them because, on a typical day, Cancers are kind, understanding, generous, loyal, and enjoy their alone time. So when they suddenly turn on a friend or become angry that they don't receive enough attention, it's quite a shock. These weaknesses can all be overcome, and it's reasonable to expect Cancers to learn how to live with them in a way that helps them build their strengths at the same time.

Unexpected Neediness

Typically, Cancers are the ones who offer emotional support for everyone around them and then retreat into their alone time for a good recharge. But occasionally, they don't retreat, and instead, want all the attention from those they love most. This unexpected change often puts people on edge because they're not sure how to handle a needy Cancer who typically needs space but now they want attention. This is very confusing for everyone else, and when a Cancer is having a bad day, that confusion, as far as they are concerned, is not *their* problem.

Cancers put up a stoic front and act like they're perfectly fine on their own and aren't reliant on anyone. But once you get close to a Cancer, you'll see the softness beneath their shell; it's clear that Cancers are high-maintenance. They're the kid that's too cool for school but really just needs a good hug and someone to show them that they don't need to present such a hard face. This weakness often comes from being overloaded or putting too much of themselves into others. Their natural inclination towards sympathy, empathy, and the need to make sure things are fair can leave them too drained to recharge on their own. They want someone to swoop in and offer comfort. Unfortunately, when they're in these moods, they're also a real Negative Nancy, which generally drives people away and worsens this mood.

So what can people, and specifically Cancers, do to handle this?

How to Overcome Neediness

Cancers can learn to manage their neediness independently, but perhaps the best approach is to have a regular regimen to offset this weakness and drive it into the dark. The way to handle this weakness is by scheduling and planning various things that will deter neediness by ensuring that the Cancer gets the attention they need from others and that they allow themselves to have alone-time.

Try the following to deter this weakness and make sure you don't unexpectedly get too needy or turn into a Negative Nancy:

- Have a weekly appointment, event, or phone call with people who can provide you with undivided attention.

- Dance and get moving to boost those feel-good hormones.

- Meditate to have time alone dedicated to processing the overwhelming feelings that you might have bottled up throughout the day.

- Watch or listen to comedy often; everyone needs to lighten up a little, and for Cancers, this should be a prescribed practice.

- Find a fun way to spend one-on-one time with another person.

Let's look at two Cancerians to see how they manage these. One male Cancer listens to a comedy talk radio while driving to and from work, or in the morning on his days off. It keeps his mood up, but also gives him something to discuss with a close friend who loves talk radio. He also has a scheduled time that he meets with his brother and a shared friend. They sit together every Friday night, sometimes at a brewery or sometimes just over pizza at one of their houses, talking and sharing until the early morning hours. It's all the attention he needs and gets him through the rest of the week as a low-maintenance Cancer.

The other Cancer is a Cancer-Leo cusp female. She's exceptionally needy, and she knows it, but it's not something she's proud of, so she puts up a front and spends a lot of time alone until finally, she snaps. Usually, she snaps once every month, or every other month if she's really doing well. But she's found that meditation can help deter the solar flares of neediness, and what helps even more is dancing. Doing it around other people helps her get attention while bonding through movement. She attends a Zumba class or does a few dance videos with a friend at home to spend time around others in a positive way. But sometimes she just needs to tell a close friend that she wants a little more one-on-one time.

Ruminating on the Past

Cancers will sit and hold on to the past. Because of their sensitivity, they'll forgive, or they say they do, but they never forget. A scar from the past is always an open wound unless they invest in recovering and re-stabilizing that relationship. This particular weakness is a sneaky one because Cancers can often benefit from spending time evaluating the past. Cancerians are highly capable of looking at what happened in the past and the changes that are happening in the present and using that information to produce a more favorable result in whatever they're doing. This goes wrong when they get into a negative spiral, which Cancers are prone to do.

Cancers can usually shed light and happiness onto situations that seem dark or foreboding to others. They're not so good at doing that for themselves. When a Cancer gets into a negative thought cycle, they can spend a lot of time looking at what they've done wrong and what situations have affected their life negatively. It's really up to them to turn this around and to pull themselves out of this negativity, but that is hard for them to do.

But why does this happen? Often ruminating on the past is a result of their ruling planet, the symbol, and their mode. The keyword that embodies a Cancer is "feeling" and that is because their ruling planet, the Moon, is responsible for emotional awareness and attunement with the soul.

Additionally, the Cancer symbol – a crab – is important because crabs molt, and in doing so they retreat into comfort often found in the past. They will also spend a lot of time holding onto key elements from the past that won't be present when developing or finding a new shell.

Finally, being a cardinal sign means that Cancers are exceptionally prone to change, and with every change comes an evaluation of past events. It is absolutely necessary for a Cancer to evaluate the past and use it to guide them into the future. Unfortunately, there is always the hazard of finding negativity in the past, and that can dramatically influence a Cancer's current mood and outlook. It is a significant weakness, but a necessary one.

How to Overcome Ruminating

One of the key factors that contribute to this weakness or bringing this weakness out is planetary movement. Typically, Cancers have a lot of control over how they deal with the past, and their openness to change allows them to move easily into the future. But certain planetary movements such as Mercury or Venus in retrograde can bring greater attention to past events that have negatively affected Cancer.

One way to work around this is to be aware of planetary movements and prepare yourself for how they will probably affect you. For example, when Venus moves into the house of Cancer, there's likely going to be an emphasis on your past romantic relationships. You might find that when Venus is in the house of Cancer, you tend to sit and think about where past loves to have gone wrong. But if you know that this is going to happen, you can embrace it and frame this in a way that's going to produce a positive result. Instead of thinking about what has gone wrong, Venus entering Cancer is the opportunity to evaluate what you took from those relationships. Even when Cancer has had an extremely negative relationship in the past, they can evaluate how they came out of that relationship as a stronger person. You can do this with each house and develop a better understanding of how a certain planet in the house of Cancer, a planet in retrograde, or part of an eclipse can impact your awareness and feelings about the past.

So, the first advice is to be aware of your birth chart and how different houses and planets impact your view of the past. The second piece of advice in handling this weakness is to document and give validity to those feelings. As a Cancer, you should already know that emotions and feelings are as real as the person who's experiencing them. Validating those feelings or acknowledging them as real gives them substantiation and allows the Cancer feeling them to move forward.

You can document and give validity to your feelings about the past by journaling, perhaps using a Voice Journal. Not everyone is comfortable putting their thoughts to paper or putting their memories down in a catalog format. Cancers can simply grab their phone or computer, open voice memos, and then speak openly. It's important to note that this is a type of emotional dumping ground. There shouldn't be any filtering or evaluation in this first part. After all the feelings are out, Cancer can then evaluate the relief of that process how they felt when they were able to get out those emotions and speak them into the universe.

Moodiness and Passive-Aggressive Nature

As a direct result of hiding their feelings, Cancers are prone to letting their feelings pile up, and then they get moody. Unfortunately, they often lash out at the people they love most, even for small problems. They can be great for months, but then they hit a point where a sink full of dishes or a minor frustration such as traffic can set them off.

Moodiness and passive aggression are possibly the biggest weakness for Cancers because this is an almost daily issue, and it largely impacts those that they're closest to. It's likely that their spouse and family members are going to be receiving the brunt of sudden mood changes and passive aggression. Don't be surprised, if you're close to a Cancer, to find snarky post-it notes or receive underhanded text messages. This can come about because of household chores, broken promises, or even things that were said months ago.

The moodiness that Cancers experience is often a result of the surrounding people. This is a downside of being an empath, someone so open to the surrounding emotions. Their passive-aggressiveness is often the Cancers trying to self-protect by not putting their emotions on their sleeve, but still addressing the underlying element of their dissatisfaction.

How to Overcome Passive Aggressive Tendencies

You shouldn't expect Cancers to make much progress in handling their moodiness or refraining from occasionally lashing out through a passive-aggressive attack. This is just a version of the-scorpion-and-the-frog syndrome; it's simply in Cancer's nature to be receptive to emotions, and that naturally produces moodiness. In a turbulent time of their life, particularly during their teenage years, there may be no hope for escaping this moodiness. Cancers need to understand how to accept and process emotions and not be overwhelmed by others. As they learn to do this, they will need time to self-reflect.

There is an opportunity for those who are close to Cancers to help. They might help by reducing how much personal expectation they put on their Cancer friend or family member. If you are a friend or spouse or family member of a Cancer, then be sure to begin your conversations with a clear outline of your expectations.

Another way that people can help Cancers avoid passive-aggressive outbursts is to acknowledge any issue on the table. Asking a Cancer what's wrong will not get you anywhere. They will probably say "nothing" and then storm off; but sitting down with them and letting them know that this is coming from a place of genuine concern can result in the conversation going much differently. Suppose you comment to a Cancer that they haven't been themselves lately, and you'd like to know why; you can start easing into the issues at hand. Make sure that you keep the conversation focused on feelings because that's where Cancers work best. Put the discussion in their hands and let them lead the way. Try asking how they've been feeling lately, or why it is that they've been acting so differently.

If you're a Cancer and would like to take a serious role in reeling in your passive-aggressive tendencies, then consider having at least one consistent creative outlet for your frustrations. Many people report a lot of success with journaling, but some people have trouble remembering to do this daily. They find themselves only journaling during either exceptionally positive or exceptionally negative moods. The idea of reeling in your moodiness means that you need to evaluate your emotional state consistently and how it may be affecting others. So if you can't journal consistently, then consider an alternative.

A few do sketching for a set amount of time each day or take a photo every day. Even just going for a five-or-ten-minute walk once a day can be your creative outlet. Think about it this way; if you take the opportunity to explore your emotions while taking time to yourself, then you won't take your frustrations out on those closest to you.

There are a thousand-and-one ways to accomplish this, and you can certainly find something that you enjoy doing every day that could give you more control over your emotions.

Ultimately, each one of these Cancerian weaknesses contributes to the whole of a Cancer's personality. Those Cancer-born are going to be far more in tune with their emotions, and have a greater understanding of other's feelings, too. You can see how these are all a natural result of the Cancerians' openness to everyone else's emotions while having to process their own. If anything, Cancers are often overwhelmed, although they keep that information to themselves. If you are a Cancer, then know you need to take time to process everything you've experienced during the day, including other people's emotions. Unless you take time for yourself to recharge, these weaknesses can easily rule over your life. Whereas taking a few steps to take care of yourself, you'll find that you're using your strengths more often than these weaknesses. If you know a Cancerian or are close to a Cancer, then be sure that you communicate clearly and don't just expect them to listen. Initiate conversations that allow

Cancer to explain their feelings and what they are going through, too. Keep in mind that Cancers tend to worry, and they may spend more time worrying over falling to these weaknesses than perhaps they should.

Chapter 5: Cancer and Planetary Movements

Planetary movements affect everyone, but they impact each sign differently. Understanding planetary movements and the objects within the universe is leaning more about science and astrology. This was the foundation of astrology, and it still largely affects how we interact with the world around us and how we feel within ourselves.

All planetary movements are taken from the earth's perspective, i.e., how they interact with the Earth's position in the universe. Each planet symbolizes different life elements or inner personality traits, but outside of the primary planets there are also special points and asteroids, often called luminaries. All of these can impact our lives directly or impact the people around us and indirectly affect our day-to-day happenings. Here are a few of the ways that planetary and luminary movements directly impact Cancerians and how to understand and accommodate the effects of these changes.

Planets and Their Relation to Cancer

Each planet represents different aspects of life, and they impact signs differently as well. There are two factors in the resulting effect; the first is that the planet enters a specific house. The second is that the person may have different experiences with that planet being in that house, as a result of their sun sign. Let's look at the relationships between your sun sign and the planetary movements in the heavens.

Mercury

Mercury in mythology is the messenger of the Gods, and so, Mercury is the planet of communication. Mercury represents not only communication but also language, intelligence, mind, and the ability to reason. Mercury takes three to four weeks to transition between signs, and retrogrades for about three weeks three or four times per year; there are a few unfortunate signs that feel the full effects of a Mercury retrograde more than the others.

Cancers often have problems with Mercury because Mercury is an unemotional planet. That lack of emotion goes directly against the core of a Cancerian personality.

For those born with Mercury in their star chart, they'll likely come across as more emotional or sensitive than they are. Mercury, however, increases the external awareness of the internal workings of a Cancer-born person.

When Mercury enters the fourth house, the house of Cancer, things get a little dicey. When Mercury is in your house, it can seem like you're overwhelmed with ideas about the past, politics, psychology, and creative pursuits. While Mercury is in your house, your emotional dissonance will often mean that you don't have the energy or clarity of thought to take action on any of these ideas.

Venus

Venus, goddess of love, ruler of Libra and Taurus, represents both love and money. People often oversimplify Venus's impact. Venus takes between four and five weeks to transition between signs. The planet goes into retrograde once every eighteen months, and it does so for about forty days, which means that it's likely to impact two signs rather than one.

This planet symbolizes the ideas of beauty, social interaction, and pleasure. For Cancers, their attachment to art, social interactions, and emotion make Venus an important planet. Venus in Cancer often provides a high level of security in relationships. Cancer's born with Venus in a prominent point in their birth chart may have underdeveloped egos, be exceptionally picky or moody in finding love, and become cold or detached as a method of self-protection. Venus entering the fourth house often means that Cancers are at the top of their game in creative endeavors and seek out social events during this time.

Mars

Representing the ancient god of war, Mars rules over Aries and transitions between signs every six or seven weeks. Mars often stirs sexual desires, competitive natures, passion, and aggression. People often say if you're going to do something big, then wait until Mars is in place. Essentially, Mars stirs our animalistic natures, which can go extremely well or absolutely terribly.

Those with Mars in Cancer on their natal chart are defensive in almost every aspect of their life and can become extremely manipulative with other's emotions. They spend extraordinary amounts of time worrying and dwelling in the past.

When Mars enters Cancer, Cancerians become extremely protective of those around them. They fear the animalistic sides that come out in people, and when it involves the house or family, they worry that people will ruin relationships or family connections. This time is when Cancers are most prone to leadership and a bit of bossiness.

Jupiter

Ruler of gods, do we need to say more? Why is Jupiter pushed to the side so often? Well, perhaps because Jupiter spends about twelve months, sometimes thirteen, in each house; it isn't often that you're directly affected, although you're always indirectly affected. In 2020, Jupiter will begin to move into Aquarius, so there are a few more years before Jupiter enters Cancer.

Jupiter represents growth, optimism, the lifestyle of abundance, and luck. Sagittarians enjoy that luck of Jupiter on a daily basis.

When Jupiter is present in the ascending position on a Cancerian's natal chart, it can help that person better manage their money and have good fortune. When it's descending in their chart, it can push them to actualize goals more often and strive for security, which may or may not come easily.

When Jupiter enters the fourth house, it places a high volume of rewards in family matters and personal happiness. People are easier to appease at home, there are fewer arguments, and people easily make warm connections.

Saturn

Ruler over Capricorn and symbolized by the Greek titan Cronus, the Father of Zeus, Saturn represents limitations and restriction. Saturn takes two or three years to transition between signs. Generally speaking, Saturn represents law, discipline, responsibility, and obligation, which all tie back to restrictions and limitations.

Saturn in the fourth house often makes everyday fun feel like a chore and chores feel like torture. Cancerians are emotion-driven, and they enjoy the freedom given by their cardinal mode and water element. Saturn takes a long time to transition houses; this doesn't happen often, but it'll last for a while when it does.

Uranus

Uranus takes seven years to transition and represents unpredictable change, eccentric appeal, rebellion, and revolution. Uranus is the god of the sky and rules over Aquarius. This house celebrates originality and scoffs at tradition. Uranus hasn't been in Cancer since 1956, but eventually it will come around again. When that happens, expect big changes in how we all understand our emotions and connect with those we love.

Now, Uranus is probably in one of your houses on your natal chart, and what you can expect is to have quite a bit of instability in that house. For example, if Uranus was in the tenth house, which traditionally rules over career, you might find that you jump from job to job, have no distinct career ambitions, and may purposefully dive into careers that seem outside of your personality.

Neptune

Ruler over Pisces and symbolizing intuition, imagination, delusions, and dreams, Neptune takes between ten and twelve years to move between signs. It's also the planet of mercy and compassion. But those with a strong Neptune presence in their star chart may also be prone to addiction, deceit, and trickery.

Pluto

Pluto takes at least twelve years to move between signs and sometimes up to fifteen years. It represents rebirth, transformation, power, and death. This planet rules over Scorpio and corresponds to Hades, the ruler of the underworld.

Pluto left Cancer most recently in 1939 and won't re-enter it any time soon. Cancers might evaluate their natal chart to identify where Pluto might affect them, and they should expect to experience fears, impulses, and big changes in that house over the course of their life.

Sun

The sun is the representation of personality, understanding of self, and ego, and is the giver of life. It influences all signs within the Zodiac in terms of people understanding themselves and connecting with their choices. It's the foundation of the sun signs and rules over Leo, who are not likely to let others forget that they're the center of the universe. It takes one month to transition between signs.

To say that the sun is in a house means that there's a special focus on that force within people's personalities. Cancerians will probably feel the strongest effects when the sun is in Cancer, and they'll tend to focus more on family and happiness.

One element that the sun provides in astrology is the idea of learning within one's self. Your sun sign is your astrological attunement; we look to the sun for answers, and those born in any given sun sign will often seek out answers to issues relating to their sun sign. Cancers will find themselves constantly learning about emotions and feelings. Cancerians have a natural drive toward curiosity about inner feelings and the emotions which drive themselves and those around them.

Mercury in Retrograde

Mercury in retrograde is one of the biggest events that happen on a regular basis when it comes to planetary movement. Mercury will go into retrograde three or four times per year and directly impact communication, which spells trouble for many people. Retrograde is when a planet is moving away from Earth, as happens when the planet laps the Earth as they are orbiting the Sun. Because Mercury completes its orbit in eighty-eight days, it is in retrograde (relative to Earth) three or four times throughout the year, and each retrograde lasts for about three weeks.

Communication

When Cancerians experience Mercury in retrograde, they really tune in to their emotions, because they are under the sign that is affected most by that particular retrograde. Mercury is not defined as masculine or feminine, but instead shape-shifts and morphs to adopt the house's characteristics. When Mercury retrograded within Cancer in 2020, it was an emotionally turbulent time for most people, but exceptionally for Cancerians, who found that they had trouble communicating with those they loved most. It affected communication and family.

But if Mercury were to retrograde in Venus, the communication troubles might only impact relationships or, specifically, new relationships. When Mercury retrogrades and impacts a house or a sign that is largely associated with tradition and stability, there's the opportunity for a positive impact. Whereas when Mercury retrogrades in an unstable or flighty sign, there are greater chances of bad news. For example, if Mercury were to retrograde in Uranus, which is largely known for unpredictable change, then you might expect every possible thing in your day-to-day life to go wrong.

No matter where Mercury is when it enters its retrograde, Cancerians should always expect an emotional overload. This overload occurs because of how many people around them feel the retrograde impact while they're also handling this struggle.

Mercury is in retrograde; a Cancer will openly be more emotional, more sensitive, and likely to lash out at those around them. They will have an uncharacteristically short temper and not have patience when it comes to communicating clearly.

Solar Eclipses

Solar eclipses are a huge deal for everyone in the Zodiac, and it doesn't matter which house the eclipse happens in, nor do the Sun and Moon signs present during the eclipse. Solar eclipses are so significant because of their rarity, and they will always affect Cancer-born people because of the presence of the moon during the eclipse.

Solar eclipses happen at the same degree within the same house every nineteen years. Because a solar eclipse took place in 2020 in Cancer, there won't be another Cancerian solar eclipse for 19 years. But every solar eclipse that takes place between now and then will still impact Cancers because, without the moon, there is no such thing as a solar eclipse.

In a nutshell, a solar eclipse is a "moon sandwich." The Moon takes a special place between the Earth and the Sun, and when it comes to astrology, that's exactly what's happening. The moon and everything it represents is eclipsing the Sun and everything it represents. Emotions and feelings take precedence over ego and self during these times.

The Moon's Phases for Cancer

Cancerians have a special issue to manage when it comes to planetary movement. They must consider that the Moon moves through the houses and that the fourth house, their house, is receptive to the effects of different planets. But they must also consider the phases of the Moon.

In astrology, the moon represents the unconscious mind, and Cancers are inherently more intuitive and connected to other people. The moon has two particular phases that directly impact Cancerians that don't impact other signs.

The moon cannot retrograde, but it can become full or new. A new moon and a full moon are excellent times for Cancers to balance home and work. It allows them to sustain a higher security and stability level than what is normally available during a waxing or waning moon.

Key points in the year involve the new moon occurring in Cancer, which happens from the end of June to the beginning of July. Then there are times when the full moon is in Cancer, which only happens from the end of December to the beginning of January. But throughout the year, as the moon waxes and wanes, it impacts Cancerians regularly.

Ongoing Planetary Tracking

Throughout this chapter, we repeatedly mentioned how planets move, and we've also mentioned a star chart or a natal chart. There are many systems online which generate a complete natal chart based on your birth information and birth location. Although you can always meet with a professional astrologist to have a complete star chart constructed for you personally, these are fairly accurate.

The star chart is your starting point and can provide a lot of insight into your personality, which goes beyond your sun and moon signs. Each planet has its own sign. Depending upon which house they were in during your birth, they will have great or little effect on you. For example, you may have been born in Cancer, you might have even been born with a Cancer moon sign as well, but if you were born with Mars in Virgo, then you may be more practical and logical than other Cancers. You might find that you naturally create systems, especially for managing the home and managing your career. That doesn't mean that you are less Cancerian, it is just another facet of your personality. It doesn't disconnect you from the water element or your emotional connection to those around you.

Now, as the planets and luminaries move throughout the heavens, those will also impact you to a certain degree. Unless you want to work closely with a professional astrologist, it's best to check planetary movement regularly through an online astrological map. These maps typically update daily and show you which house the Moon is in, which house your moon sign is in, and other planetary movement elements that might impact you, such as Mercury in retrograde. Because Cancerians are so in tune with the world around them and others' emotions, they can often benefit more than others when it comes to ongoing planetary tracking. Cancer-born people are extremely receptive to those around them, so a nearby Aquarius or

Taurus having something impactful in their star chart could affect the Cancers in their life. Be aware of and receptive to planetary tracking.

Chapter 6: The Cancerian Child

Eventually, everyone spends time thinking about or reflecting on their childhood. They might do this well into adulthood or even start the evaluation process as a teen. Cancers often experience their best qualities in their most heightened state as children. Cancerian children can be a pleasure to raise, but they can be extremely emotional and flip from one emotion to another in a matter of seconds. It's not simply because they're an emotion-driven sign.

These mood fluctuations happen because Cancer children are very receptive to the changes in planetary positions and changes within the universe. When a planet goes into retrograde or into a new house, Cancerian children will often feel the response to that before any other sign, at any other age.

As a quick overview, a Cancer baby or child is sympathetic and intuitive, but they require a lot of extra attention. Cancer children are often very demanding until they hit an age where they begin to explore their creative and imaginative side. As Cancer children begin to understand and grab hold of their imagination, they become very independent.

Understanding Yourself as a Child

What were you like as a child? Well, if you were born under the Cancer sign, then you were probably prone to be a bit stubborn, throw the occasional tantrum, and as an older child leading into your preteen years, probably spent quite a bit of time entertaining yourself. Of course, things like the first order, the signs of your parents, and your siblings' signs can all play a role in how Cancer children grow and develop.

What Cancer children can repeatedly deliver into any family unit is a spark of light. It goes right back to the moon being the only entity in the universe that can reflect the light of the sun. Cancer children may experience slumps or feel like they're in a rut, but they are often very concerned about keeping others happy. You may have sacrificed quite a bit as a child for the benefit of others, even for keeping adults in your life happy. This is often particularly true of firstborns in the family or children that have a large age gap over their younger siblings. Firstborn Cancers, both male and female, are often prone to developing their leadership skills earlier in life and will probably seek out leadership roles in their adult career.

Cancers that are middle children are more likely to be a bit sulky. Whereas middle children are often known for their outbursts, Cancers are more withdrawn and shyer. It's likely that they'll actively seek out love rather than attention, and as children, they'll quickly cultivate a tight-knit friend group that they'll keep for a long stretch of time.

I can see when Cancers are the baby of the family. They are that free kindred spirit. They might seem reserved, but they're certainly not as shy as other Cancer children. These children will often develop deep and intimate relationships with your family members, and they're definitely the type of children to see their older siblings as heroes.

It's likely that regardless of your birth order, you had very nurturing qualities as a child. This is seen in Cancers that have had a very hard childhood as well as Cancers that have had a really easy childhood. They generally enjoy time alone but really want to spread that love and affection to the people around them. Sometimes Cancer children do this to their own detriment, where they may be giving more love than they're receiving, or they may find themselves constantly craving the attention of the person in the family who shows the least interest in them. Cancer children can have trouble building self-confidence and trying new things. It can initially seem like a setback, but many Cancerians blossom during the later teenage years.

What Cancer Children Need

So, what do Cancer children really need to thrive? Regardless of the parent's sign, there are a few things that parents of Cancer children should do to address the Cancerian needs specifically. First, they need to make sure that they're giving enough attention to this child. Even if you received a ton of attention as a child, you might have had that constant want for more. Children that are born to the fourth house are often under this insatiable appetite for attention and praise.

It can get to the point where Cancer children just want to sit next to somebody or watch TV together. They don't necessarily need a lot of one-on-one, hands-on time but they need a lot of quiet time together.

As Cancerian children develop, they need a bit of space. Their privacy becomes very important to them, especially between the ages of five to nine. As Cancers go through childhood, they go through more of an emotional journey than other children. While they certainly need mental and physical nourishment as well as family time, there are emotions that they are just going to have to learn how to process on their own. For many children, this emotional journey as a Cancer can seem really taxing. You might notice that they often nap or turn to sedentary hobbies such as watching TV rather than sports.

If you're a Cancer, you might remember being told constantly that you needed to go outside, that you needed to be spending more time with friends, or that you need to play with siblings. Although it's frustrating hearing these things as a child, that is exactly what I call childhood. A parent is going to help pull them out of their shell so they can become comfortable in trying new things on their own. It can also help Cancer children develop social skills early in childhood where they might otherwise stagnate. Catholic children are well known for their ability to make it in life, and when they make a friend, it's often lifelong. But they get into a pattern of, once they make one or two good friends, not socializing outside of that immediate circle.

In short, Cancer children need nourishment and encouragement. Parents of Cancer children should focus on helping them develop skills that can offset certain Cancer weaknesses such as moodiness and the inclination to be alone. They should also put direct effort into providing the attention needed to nurture a Cancer and the space they need to digest the day or particularly troublesome events. As a result of Cancer's empathetic abilities and emotional receptiveness, it's possible that even a family disagreement could result in the Cancer child needing time alone after a bit of cuddling or special attention.

Parenting a Cancerian

So many people wonder how exactly they can parent a Cancerian child when they're so emotional and needy. They're emotional and intense, and often parents feel lost or as though they can't get anything right.

As infants, you might feel completely drained because they constantly need to have a good cuddle. These children may be impossible to put down. After you get through that first hard year of infancy, you can see the Cancer child flourish, and parents of a Cancer will need to pivot. Parents of Cancers need to be authoritative from a distance. Their child needs a physical connection with their parents, but they may demand too much or use their needs to evade discipline.

Here's an example of a typical Cancer child interaction:

The child picks up an item they shouldn't have.

Mom: Put that down right now.

The child puts the item down.

Mom: Thank you.

The child picks up the item again.

Mom: Put that down.

Child: But mom...

Mom: Put it down, or timeout.

Child: Mom, please.

Mom takes away the item.

The child doesn't cry but instead hugs the parent. It's a form of manipulation that children use unintentionally. But this is a prevalent technique used by Cancer children. When other children would get mad, Cancer children become apologetic or even act as though they're experiencing shame for not complying or not appeasing the authority figure. That is why parents need to be authoritative from a distance. Clearly, parents need to set boundaries and take actions for safety, such as taking away potentially harmful items or having rules in place like not walking in the street. But how do you enforce these when your child only wants more attention and love after being scolded? Parents for Cancers have to be strong and lead communication. When you're calm, and the child has had an opportunity to process the interaction without getting immediate "forgiveness," then you can both talk. Because Cancers are so empathetic and receptive, Cancer children can often have deeper discussions than most children. When parenting a Cancer, don't shy away from emotionally intense discussions or explaining your feelings; it can help the child overcome stubbornness and understand their sympathetic nature.

A word of caution, Cancer children are more likely to fit into assigned labels. If you tell a Cancer child that they're "bad," they'll feel that way. If you tell them that they're a "bully" or "stubborn," they will be toward that behavior even though it hurts.

Cancer Teens

Teenagers come with emotional turbulence, but a Cancer teen is an outright conundrum that absolutely baffles parents. Sometimes they'll want to spend more time with their family than anyone would ever imagine from a teenager. The next day they're picking fights with everyone. No one is safe from this hormonal, emotional, irrational, loving, and kindhearted person.

Cancer teens demand privacy, and when a parent or sibling violates privacy boundaries or quiet time, they feel outright betrayed. Don't search a Cancer teen's room or get into their items without an invitation. It's probable that you won't find much, anyway. Typically, Cancer children will keep their friends right into their teenage years. Their friends may fall into bad habits or shady situations, but if not, great; you can pretty much count on a Cancer teen sticking around with people they know.

When it comes to simple check-ins, a "How was your day?" question can set red flags off in a Cancer teen's head. If you're prying too much, they'll just become more secretive and retreat from the parent.

What you can expect from a Cancer teen is a high level of motivation. It may not necessarily be for school, but they'll find a passion, and it'll likely follow them all through life; and, it's probably for one of the arts. Cancer teens are often leaders among their peers if they're passionate about local news or activism.

How can you help a Cancer teen develop? Here are some ways to help them grow and flourish:

- *Allow them personal responsibility.* Ask them to cook one night a week or take on a task to make their own.

- *Acknowledge how they help the family.* Cancers can have all different types of love languages, and as a teen, it can be hard to pin down that teen's preferred language. Maybe fit a few different approaches for appreciation into your day. Say "thank you", offer an incentive or reward for their efforts, pick up one of their chores, or do something special for them once in a while.

- *Drop unnecessary rules.* Cancer teens tend to rebel against nonsense or anything that they don't feel is important. Don't set an arbitrary bedtime for no particular reason, and make curfews dependent on the situation. For example, instead of saying "Remember that your curfew is 11:00 p.m.", you can say, "Oh, it's prom night, you'll probably be out late. Let's make it before 1:00 this time." Or, for example, "If you can't get home from John's house before 10:00, ask if you can stay the night." That way, they don't have the sword of Damocles hanging over their head at every turn.

- *Indulge their self-expression.* As with any teen, they're figuring out their personal preferences, what they like and dislike. Because Cancers are so emotional, this is a little more important here than with other teenagers. Avoid comments that put down their personal preferences without any good reason. For example, "You call that music?", or "I can't stand that, turn it down." In both instances, you can ask for the volume to go down without asserting that you don't like what they like. Cancer teens still crave that connection to their family, and they want to have a connection with you; they don't want to hear that you hate something they love.

Cancerians as Parents

We couldn't leave a chapter about Cancerian children without some discussion of Cancers as parents. Cancerian parents are widely celebrated as the best nurturers in the Zodiac. They're not just great parents because they're intuitive and empathetic; it's because they remember exactly what it was like to grow up as a sensitive and emotional child. Cancers have the innate ability to hold on to the past, and they don't forget the hurts or the joys of childhood.

This particular element is one of the few places where male and female Cancers really differ. Cancerian fathers are the fun parents, the ones who let the kids stay up late and eat junk food, the ones who can connect with them on an emotional level. They protect their children and can be fierce if they're threatened. But, as much as they're a papa bear or daddy crab, they also want to be their children's friend and to shower them with affection.

Female Cancers make prize mothers. They're the loving authority that nurtures and/or disciplines as the situation demands. They're overprotective, and on occasion can be a bit overbearing. Often, they love the labor of mothering, and they're the type to have a fully loaded schedule with shuttling kids to all sorts of activities. They tend to remember from childhood how their parents did or did not encourage creative exploration and self-explanation.

If you grew up as a Cancer child, take pride in knowing that you can give your children that dream childhood of affection, connection, and provoking constant growth. You might have had a hard run through the teenage years, but they prepared you for everything that you would face through adult years. The emotional ebb and flow often subsides in the later teens and allows Cancers to take all their lessons learned through childhood to become the best parents.

Chapter 7: Cancer in Love

Cancers are often applauded as the best lovers in the Zodiac. They are sensual, emotional, and passionate, which seems like a recipe for success in any romantic relationship. Unfortunately, they also tend to be a bit needy, but that is something that any sign in the Zodiac can adjust to in consideration of what they're getting from the Cancer person.

Cancers surprisingly have quite a bit of trouble when it comes to love, and there's a clear reason for it. Let's address this challenge in romance before we dive into what a Cancer is like when they find their mate.

While Cancers are certainly the best lovers in the Zodiac, they often can't find another sign that can reciprocate that level of love, compassion, and emotional connection. It might seem like the solution is that Cancers need to find other Cancers, but typically Cancers aren't compatible because of how needy they can be and how much they crave alone time. With Cancer-Cancer relationships, it's common that they struggle to be on the same wavelength because they're both exceptionally receptive, but also demanding. Later on, we'll discuss Cancer's compatibility with each sign, but know that typically, the Cancer-Cancer connection isn't the simple solution for

Cancers receiving the love they need. Another avenue that Cancer's often find themselves on is to connect with a fire sign, which we'll evaluate individually as well, as these relationships are either made for the stars or absolute disaster.

Ultimately, Cancers have epic romances, and they're deserving of only the best. When they share too much of themselves, they are at risk of being overrun. Their natural inclination toward leadership makes them likely to dominate a relationship, but they're looking for someone to guide the way toward happiness in a partner. Relationships for Cancers are usually wonderful or tumultuous.

"Catching Feelings" is Fairly Literal for Cancers

The slang term "catching feelings" almost exactly describes how Cancers fall in love. They start talking to someone, and then suddenly, they don't just have a crush, they're head over heels. It's a vortex for Cancers, they love *love*. They love other people and experiencing the emotions of a new romance. Their sensuality and understanding of emotions make them fall hard and easily.

Cancers are exceptionally attuned when it comes to love and their physical sensations. When it comes to sex, Cancers want to have nearly an act of worship, and they start thinking about it early on. Most Cancers don't pounce on the idea of moving too quickly on the physical side. But when it comes to emotions, they are often found *running* into relationships, or at least fantasizing about it. The joke about imagining a wedding after that first message is particularly true for Cancers. They're dreamers with lots of love to give, and they hope to receive a lot of love in return.

When it comes to dating, Cancers can be a bit cagey. They like getting to know people, and sometimes the relationship can stagnate and result in great friendships but no relationship. Cancers may also enjoy the dating process and continue that element of the pursuit deep into their relationship, making for a truly fruitful relationship. They love discovering, but Cancers ultimately want to find long-term, slow-burning love in comfortable, low-stress settings.

Intimacy and Physical Love

When in bed, Cancers make long and passionate love. They aren't the ones to bring in toys, shower sex, or props. They want an act of passion approaching worship. Cancers want eye contact, cuddling, and lazy days spent in bed. A lot of these tendencies play into the Cancerian water element. There's a ton of intimacy, but it's reserved for a few in most cases. Cancers aren't usually promiscuous, although they love getting to know people and might occasionally dip into isolated bouts of promiscuity.

Cancer Women and Cancer Men in Relationships

"Mars... Venus", and all the other business, but the undeniable fact is that men and women are different. It's hard to argue that they're overly different, emotionally and psychologically, but Cancer men and women have separate ways of expressing their needs when it comes to love and romance.

Cancer men tend to be soft, loving, and occasionally nurturing, but you have to put in a lot of hard work to get through that shell. They protect themselves at all costs, which means that a partner might get used to a low-maintenance, highly independent partner only to hit the level of trust necessary for the Cancer man to unleash his softer side. Cancer men often believe in chivalry but may be apt to hide this as they know that their partner might crave higher independence levels or even put off by traditional romance or courting.

It's important to address the fact that Cancer men are easily hurt, and if they're hurt once, they're not apt to forget it. One misstep could mean the end of the relationship, or it taking weeks or even months to rebuild lost trust.

Cancer women in love are the true moon maidens. They want to be wooed and romanced... but, Cancer women take a bit of time to warm up. They are generally stand-offish and suspicious of potential partners. They don't want to get hurt, but they also don't want to waste their time. Unfortunately, for all their suspicion and guardedness, many will find themselves giving much more in a relationship than they'll get out of it.

Because Cancer women, like Cancer men, are self-protective but also ruled by feelings, they do a good job of hiding emotions that they think aren't welcome in the relationship. The Cancer woman specifically may keep a lot of her emotions to herself until she reaches a breaking point and then unleashes a hurricane of emotion. They aren't the crazy girlfriend; if the partner makes it past that initial hurricane, they should have smooth waters ahead (unless they don't learn their lesson, in which case the relationship may be doomed or at least off to a rocky start).

Cancer Compatibility

Overall, Cancers have a high compatibility rate. Here's the overview for each sign's compatibility with Cancer and the specifics about what to expect in these different relationships.

Cancer and these signs have the highest level of compatibility:

Taurus

The Taurus is a steadfast and passionate lover, which can work out quite well. As a fixed sign, they can help ground a Cancer man or woman, and they're likely to catalyze intense physical chemistry.

Pisces

Cancer and Pisces will have an intense ride, but it can be magic if they meet each other at the right point in life. A mentally mature Cancer and a mentally mature Pisces can make lifelong mates that have a nearly unmatched emotional connection. They dream together, plan together, and share that bond for years.

Scorpio

Two water signs that are meant for each other, there's a magnetism that draws these two together. Even when epic fights happen, it certainly doesn't mean the end of the relationship is near. The emotional eruptions are just part of these two signs being together. Fighting could be an outlet that allows them to appreciate each other more once their emotions stabilize.

Aries

Expect well-matched intimacy but little else. This fire sign is the "dry" fire sign and the least compatible with any water signs, but especially with Cancer. The communication in these relationships takes a lot of effort. Is it impossible? No, but it takes work from both sides.

Gemini

Cancers and Geminis get along quite well, and if you're looking for a love that has a foundation of friendship, this could be it. Don't expect as much passion in the bedroom but enjoy the open communication.

Cancer

This could be the best or worst relationship you might have as a Cancer. It's possible that you find someone you click with and that you're emotionally aligned to, or it could turn out that one of you is always on opposite ends of the emotional spectrum.

Leo

As the pure fire sign, Leos offer Cancers a chance at a passionate and steamy romance. Leo's are egotistical and can have trouble communicating, but they can shower love the same way that Cancers do in a relationship. It's important that the Leo and the Cancer work out who is the leader in the relationship.

Virgo

Virgos are highly compatible, but they can be combative with Cancers when it comes to emotional demands. Virgos are generally very private people, and that works out well when Cancers want their space. But then there are those other times.

Libra

There are few signs that don't fit well with Libras, and there are few signs that don't play well with Cancers. These two seem like they'd be perfect as they're both kind-hearted and concerned with fairness, but they don't mix well. Cancers are too good at sniffing out fakeness, and Libras aren't happy to handle an emotional rollercoaster.

Sagittarius

These two will have tons of fun together, but probably not result in a long-lasting relationship unless the lighthearted Sagittarius can accommodate Cancer's ever-changing mood. And of course, unless the Cancer can keep up with the wild Sagittarius ambitions.

Capricorn

There's high compatibility here and a moderate level of communication. You shouldn't have any problems easing into a steady relationship with a Capricorn so long as you both remember that you're prone to quiet bouts.

Aquarius

Expect almost no communication here. While Cancers are great listeners and Aquarians are great talkers, these two just don't align when it comes to delivery. Of course, there is an opportunity to overcome communication hurdles, but generally, the air and water combination is a little lackluster for the emotional Cancer.

Water and Earth

Water and earth mixtures are more like the edge of the beach than the mud that people imagine. These signs include Taurus, Capricorn, and Virgo. Cancer has the ability to soften a few of these signs, which are typically very reserved and private. But in doing that they may open a box of emotions they weren't prepared to handle.

There should be a balance between earth signs offering practical help and encouragement, with the Cancer leading communication efforts.

Water and Fire

Water and fire signs are passion bottled up until the top blasts off. It's a steamy combination that can be all right or all wrong. There are particular issues with the fire signs as they're a bit different from the other elements. Fire signs include Aries, the hot moving toward dry, Leo the pure fire sign, and Sagittarius the hot moving toward wet.

Typically, a Cancer doesn't have much to gain besides intimacy or friendship from an Aries or Sagittarius. There's either a lot of passion or a lot of fun. With Leo, there's the opportunity for a relationship, but it could be disastrous.

There's also the risk that a fire sign could make the water sign feel dried up, that they may not receive the nourishment they need. At the same time, fire signs may feel that the water signs douse their burning inspiration.

All the same, Cancers frequently jump into relationships with fire signs because the feelings and emotions at the start of the relationship are too intense to turn down.

Water and Air

When it comes to water and air, you almost couldn't ask for a deeper connection until we get to water and water combinations. Air signs create a strong foundation for water to communicate their feelings and dream lofty dreams. These signs often feed off of each other very well and encourage each other to move forward. The downside is that these are often friendships, and sometimes cultivating the communication with Cancer opens up emotions, and air signs aren't always stable when it comes to long-term commitment.

Water and Water

Now, water and water are a match made in heaven. After all, we're looking to cultivate an ocean, not be a lonesome pond. But there's a bit of challenge because sometimes these couples see too much of themselves in their partner. They'll need to understand when their partner wants alone time, and when they can merge together and spark their emotional bond.

How to Catch a Cancer's Eye

It sounds like such a cliché, but you really just need to be yourself. Cancers are too empathetic and perceptive to be fooled by manipulation. If someone is doing anything but being authentic, even if they're just trying to play it cool, a Cancerian can tell. So, don't ever try to manipulate or fool a Cancer; they can always tell.

Then, make time for them. If you manage to land a date, know that you might have to do a fair amount of the talking. But filling the air with conversation doesn't mean that you're running the show. Make time for them and direct the conversion in a way that invites them to do more than just listen; offer engagement. Additionally, it's best to ensure that this one-on-one time is distraction-free. Grab a meal and talk. But leave your phone and other devices off or on silent. Cancers hate to break the mood when they're in the getting-to-know-each-other phase.

Finally, have real conversations. Don't talk about surface topics like the weather, traffic, or the latest shows. Cancers are excellent conversationalists, but they don't often employ that skill because they're such great listeners. Finding someone who draws out this element in their personality is something really exciting, and Cancers love to explore people and even themselves. Give them a chance.

So, how should you approach Cancer? Start direct. They don't like muddled communication. If you like them, say so, and then give them a bit of space but don't fully disconnect. Chat through the day or a few times a week, making sure that you don't come on too strong or abandon them completely.

How to Communicate with Your Partner if You're a Cancer

If you're a Cancer, you might have noticed through this chapter that any time there were genuine troubles, it was due to communication. Communication plays a vital role in every relationship, romantic or otherwise, but when dealing with a partner, it's vital that you keep those lines of communication open. Cancers do have a tendency to shut down unintentionally, and often their partners can perceive that as getting the silent treatment.

Look for everyday ways to communicate, and when you can't find the words, send images, gifs, or even memes. Embrace text messaging, and send video messages; that way, you don't have to video chat, but instead, you can send a personal message without worrying about having a full conversation.

You might also consider being blunter than what seems normal or polite. Cancers like to ease into discussing their feelings because they're so wrapped up in everyone else's. If you're feeling mad, flustered, or needing attention, then be blunt about it rather than trying to keep that emotion buried. Only when Cancerians don't address their needs, especially emotional needs, do they have these blow-up fights with their partners or mates. It's likely that any problem in a relationship involving a Cancer and anyone else has its root in unaddressed emotions. Address the emotions you're experiencing directly, rather than trying to address the other person's needs first.

Finally, give some consideration to their sign. The compatibility outline above is a general guide, but if you're both aware of your strengths and weaknesses, you can have a successful relationship with signs that may initially seem incompatible. Romantic relationships rely on personalities coming together and two people being interdependent, which is possible in a variety of combinations. But if you're with someone who is refusing to work through difficult communication or understanding emotional needs, then it's not likely you'll see any substantial change in the relationship itself. Seeking out strong relationships is something that Cancers are very good at. They're often very content being independent until they find someone with whom they can be themselves and enjoy the time.

Chapter 8: Cancers at a Party

From the outside, Cancerians are walking conundrums. Many other signs see them as simply impossible to understand, and one of the reasons for this is their varying degrees of social interactions. Again, from the outside Cancers seem like introverts, but on the inside Cancerians know that they not only love a good party, they love hosting one. Cancer-born people often feel drained when they're around extreme emotions, but they usually enjoy the happy vibes at a party.

Cancerians also enjoy a bit of pampering and attention from time to time. Cancers tend to spend more time at a party with a small group of people, and when they're hosting, they make sure they're not spreading themselves too thin. Overall, it's surprising, but Cancers love to party, and they love social interaction when they can control part of the environment. Here are a few of the deeper insights into how Cancerians enjoy time around others and what they can do to make the most of that time.

Cancers Party to Unwind

Cancers have two ways of unwinding. The first is the more notable, and the more gossiped about, need for seclusion. Cancerians do like to hide away from the world; it's very crab-esque of them. But they are just as likely to host a small get-together and use that as an opportunity to recharge. In fact, this is one of the best ways for Cancer-born people to learn to overcome their most prominent weaknesses.

Because Cancers are so easily affected by others' emotions, they have trouble separating the good from the bad in many situations.

Think about it for a minute... when you go to work, you probably get a mix of good and bad emotions. You might have a coworker who's excited for a big trip with their family and another coworker who feels like he's stuck in a dead-end job and hates his life. Cancers pick up on both of these. But a party with people you know and love is a different experience.

Throwing a party with your closest loved ones has a high probability of turning out a good time and everyone being happy. That's why Cancers love a good get-together, but they're not one for raging parties.

If you're trying to imagine a Cancer having a great time at a party and being able to unwind, then think of more of a kicked-back affair as opposed to a frat party. We're talking about a bit of barbecue, maybe casual drinking, and really good conversation. When Cancers party, they don't have music that drowns out conversation, or the focus itself is on the music and the conversation is about what's playing. They do best when they're offering home-cooked meals to their friends and spending time around people they know they'll enjoy.

Now, a Cancer-Leo cusp might find more enjoyment in the big party scene. They might plan out these experiences well ahead of time to ensure that they can emotionally prepare but being extremely social is one of those characteristics that come out in the Cancer-Leo cusp. These people might find greater joy in planning to attend a big event such as a well-established rave, concert, or seasonal event. Even those people who fall on the Gemini-Cancer cusp will probably enjoy partying for the sake of fun more than pure Cancers. But both Gemini-Cancer and Cancer-Leo cusps should expect the same recharge effective when attending small gatherings.

Prefer Consistency Over Novelty

Male Cancers are prone to enjoying parties more than female Cancers are. They're traditionalists, and they understand that socializing is part of regular life. They want to plan their social encounters, and in doing so it may seem like they're setting up a very old-school-style affair. It's likely them, a few male friends, moderate drinking, background music, and reserved for Friday or Saturday night. Their innately loyal nature and dependability often mean that these consistent and traditional get-togethers happen regularly. The friends of this Cancer likely know to show up every Saturday night whether they receive an invitation or not. In fact, a Cancer might occasionally take the liberty of not sending invites to see who shows up anyway.

Even female Cancers prefer to party with a bit of consistency over novelty. These are not the type of people who want to go with other people's spur-of-the-moment ideas, but female Cancers are known for occasional spontaneous streaks. They are typically less traditional than male Cancers and tend to use their imaginative or creative side more often when seeking fun. These moments of spontaneity aren't the crazy "let's go jump off the bridge" situations; they're usually just last-minute plans. It's likely that a female Cancer will realize she has an empty weekend and invite over a few close friends.

It's likely that female Cancers also have standing plans with the most important people in their life. For many, that is something to the extent of a Sunday dinner, Friday date night, or after-work drinks with coworkers. It's this degree of consistency that allows the Cancer to unwind and relax with people that she enjoys being around frequently. There's often too much uncertainty for either a male or female Cancer to enjoy themselves when it comes to novelty. You can expect that Cancerians aren't really big on theme parks or summer festivals unless they can plan out all the details and/or create a consistent schedule. For example, a Cancerian might not want a one-time trip to Disneyland. But, if they live in Southern California or Florida, they might get a season pass so they can go as often as they like and do things at their own pace. They would not use these outings as a party and would likely shut down the idea of using highly eventful or hyped-up locations for parties such as family get-togethers or class reunions.

Cancers When Party Planning and Hosting

Although Cancers seem shy, there's a lot that they manage when it comes to socializing. Part of that comes from a need to control new interactions, but they are good at slowly growing their circle of friends and often mix friend groups when others would keep them separate. Because of this, they seem like that one person that knows everyone, and everyone knows them.

But planning and hosting are exceptionally demanding, and it's one of those triggers that can set off moodiness, frustration, and a full Cancer shut down. Cancers work best as mediators and orchestrators. They are the ones who make the right decision when it comes down to a few choices, but when they have to go out and find all the options, research them, and make the decision, things go wrong. Decision paralysis or decision fatigue is common among party-planning Cancers.

On the fun side, we can say that Cancers should grab a glass of Pinot Grigio and enjoy a weekend at the winery rather than a Friday night at the bar. We can also say that Cancers are rather sensuous, and they want a head-to-toe pampering experience. A good salt scrub and a hot shower followed by a full body massage would do just the trick for Cancer-born individuals.

These are the fun things that you find in magazines about how to find the best spa package or the best cocktail to make your weekend stand out. The truth is that Cancers don't need all of this. They aren't the ones looking for things that are just right; if anything, they're looking for elements of the parties that are just right for everyone else. They're the ones who are likely to make a menu and/or a drink menu and contrive the entertainment based on what they think everyone else would enjoy. Never forget that Cancer-born are the mothering archetype of the Zodiac, and they don't just want to nurture; they want to deliver a happy experience.

If you're a Cancer who wants to entertain more often or enjoys entertaining, then take the leap and get help. Ask a friend and use those Cancer charms to get the help that people want to give. You listen, and you know what people want and how they are best capable when it comes to helping. Say to your friend, "You always have the best games at the kids' parties, could you help with this party?" Or "Hey, what do you think would be great for our Saturday bar-b-cue? You know good food!"

Again, Cancers want to use a party's opportunity to draw out those good emotional vibes and enjoy everyone around them being in a good mood. They don't want the planning process or the party itself to feel like a chore, and to avoid that, they'll often ask for help to put together a party or to ensure that things go as planned. It's one of the few times that Cancerians ask for help, and they certainly deserve it!

Who is the Cancer at a Party?

If you were to try to ascertain each person of the Zodiac Trope at a hypothetical party, then the Cancer would be the one sitting outside by the fire pit. You'll likely find them with a couple of close friends, but they're not going to be the ones circulating and talking with people that they don't know or aren't comfortable around. Additionally, Cancers are likely the ones who are going to call it an early night (unless they're hosting the party). When Cancers are hosting the party, they don't mind it going well into the early morning hours. But when a

Cancer knows that they have the opportunity to go home and genuinely unwind, they'll take it.

All too often, other signs feel like Cancers aren't happy at parties. They don't understand that even if a Cancer is just sitting outside quietly with one or two friends and food, they're having a good time. Cancers are not the ones who are going to have a good time getting up on the bar and dancing. They're also not the ones who are going to have a lot of fun from typical party games.

It's also likely that Cancers are quick to put down ideas for parties that seem more like a novelty. Things like gender reveal, baby showers, wedding rehearsal parties, and anything else that seems superfluous won't be at the top of a Cancer's priority list. The one exception to this is if the Cancer is planning or hosting the party for someone they love. That mothering and caring instinct will drive them to throw parties that they believe the person who is the focus of the festivity will enjoy. Even if they're not keen on the idea of the party, they'll usually go along with it to make another person happy.

Chapter 9: Cancers at Work and Career Paths

Cancers are especially industrious people. As a water sign, they're able to employ their mystery, creativity, and kind-heartedness in their work. Their sensitivity and high level of intuition can lead to trouble in finding the right career path and following through.

The characteristics of a Cancer make them a hard-working, loyal, and exceptionally diligent employee. These people will pay attention to very specific rules and have that keen eye for detail that many employers love. When they take on a professional role, it's a commitment. Cancerians are not the type to move from job to job frequently. It's likely that even when they feel ready to move on, they'll stay for an additional year or two, feeling that they owe their employer something.

How do Cancerians Act with Their Coworkers?

As coworkers, Cancers tend to lean one of two ways. They're either the energetic and positive force on the team that encourages others to reach new success levels or the opposite. It's important not to forget how moody Cancer can be at times. Suppose they feel jaded or underappreciated in the workplace. In that case, it's often that they're the ones on the team pointing out the negative aspects of the work environment with little insight into how to solve these problems. Cancers work best with a bit of autonomy, but they don't enjoy working alone. They need to work with a team of people they believe are competent, but who contribute differently. It's not enough to have a team of nice people. Cancers want to work on a team of forward-thinking people who contribute new ideas, even if they don't particularly agree with them. Cancers want everyone to explore their creativity, and they do tend to bring this out in other people. But, if you're a Cancer yourself, you might know all too well that this is only the outside perspective. To your coworkers, you're possibly an outstanding team member who is supportive and helps the team grow. But that may come with a deep internal struggle to be heard and to communicate what you have to contribute to the team. There are often two ways of looking at things, from the inside and the outside. For Cancers in the workplace, every day has this divide. Cancerians must find a career path or at least an employer that they truly enjoy. As an emotionally-driven Cancer, taking a job that makes you unhappy is not a long-term option.

In what type of jobs might Cancers perform best and find personal satisfaction? As natural caregivers and counselors, Cancers thrive in roles that allow them to help other people. That doesn't always mean that they're going to be a nurse or professional caregiver, although those are both excellent careers for Cancerians. It might be in a role that helps people help themselves, such as teaching or working in management. Additionally, many Cancers find satisfaction in providing help in everyday ways by working as a mechanic or an electrician. The overwhelming suggestion that you'll find for a Cancer career path is that they should lean towards the arts. Unfortunately, although creative, many Cancers struggle in artistic careers because they're not achieving satisfaction through other elements of their personality. If you have an artistic inclination or want to pursue a career in an artistic field, then make sure that you surround yourself with ways of expressing your kind-heartedness, generosity, and desire to do good for other people.

Realtor

It's a bit of a shock to recommend a Cancer work as a realtor, but there are a great many ways that Cancers thrive in real estate. First and foremost, they're helping people find a home, and that's not something that many people can say they've accomplished. Secondly, real estate is more of an art than a science. You have to know what your client wants and what they expect even when they can't describe it themselves.

A new couple may say that they want a simple starter home within their budget and mentioned that they're planning on growing their family quickly. When handling this, a Cancer may recognize that yes, they do want a starter home. But they also want a house with enough bedrooms for multiple children and probably an extra bathroom.

Furthermore, working as a real estate agent provides the perfect level of teamwork and autonomous work. Real estate agents are almost always independent contractors, but they work with a real estate broker's office and use collective resources. It's likely that as a realtor, you'll participate in weekly team meetings and be called upon for expertise if one of your teammates is having trouble with a sale or with paperwork.

Overall, working as a real estate agent allows Cancers the opportunity to develop themselves, work with others, genuinely help their clients, and guide people through a process that they may only go through once or twice in their life. Working as a real estate agent allows Cancers the opportunity to develop themselves, work with others, genuinely help their clients, and guide people through a process that they may only go through once or twice in their life.

Chef

Working as a chef is the first artistic career path mentioned on this list. Earlier it was mentioned that working as an artist, musician, comedian, or writer might not exactly fit Cancers. Simply producing creative work isn't enough for Cancers. Instead, they should find a profession that allows their Cancer traits to thrive while they also explore their creative inclinations. Chefs do exactly do that. Often, Cancers can get substantial personal satisfaction from crafting delicious meals for people.

We're not talking about your run-of-the-mill cook. If you're looking to be a chef, it's best to get formal education or training but with a celebrated chef if at all possible. We're talking about working your way into restaurants that people go to feel good, rather than blasting through a drive-through for something to ease a bit of hunger.

We're not talking about your run-of-the-mill cooks. If you're looking to be a chef, it's best to get formal education or training under a celebrated chef, if it all possible. We're talking about working your way into restaurants that people go to for a fine dining experience, rather than blasting through a drive-through for something to ease a bit of hunger. Explore your artistic abilities while delivering outstanding performance in this sometimes thankless profession.

Interior Design or Design Professional

An interior-design professional helps people take an average house and make it a lovely home. Cancers love helping, they love crafting, and they usually enjoy creating beautiful things. There's a strong sense of reward when they're able to finish a job.

Unlike the realtor profession, most interior designers don't work in an office with other people who work independently as well. Instead, interior designers are usually independent contractors entirely on their own, or underlings to another designer's operation. Keep in mind that Cancers are natural leaders, and in creative pursuits probably won't do well just taking directions from another person (unless they're new to the field and deliberately engaged in learning). Cancers are often passionate about learning, so taking the lead from a respected person in the field isn't a problem in that situation. But taking the lead from another person when the Cancer simply wants to exercise their passion, creativity, and desire to explore, doesn't suit them well.

You might have the option to open your own design firm or work freelance, finding clients on your own. In many cases, you might find a work partner, who should be a good friend that can work with your clients while you design away.

Social Worker

It's no surprise that Cancers should be in the recommended service field when it comes to social work. Social workers have the ability to deliver actual help to families and children, rather than just mandate reports to alert the proper offices of their suspicions.

Social work also explores another area unique to Cancers. They're often attracted to mystery because they're a water sign and the ocean contains its own air of mystery, and as a social worker, there's quite a bit of opportunity to investigate and research.

Nurse or Caregiver

Nursing and caregiving is hard work, there's no doubt about it, but Cancers never shy away from hard work. Imagine long hours of helping people, jumping into emergency situations and high-stress environments with a calm cool because you're the one that's there to help.

Cancers that are high-energy might enjoy nursing more than caregiving. They may have more reliable schedules that offer a bit more flexibility with three days off, even though it means working twelve-hour shifts or being on-call through the rest of the week. Longer stretches of time off also allow Cancerians the opportunity to recharge fully, where other jobs might not offer that same benefit.

As a caregiver, Cancers can get too receptive to their patients' emotional despondence and that of the family members that do or don't appear. Cancers are almost always natural empaths, and it can be hard to find so much sadness or grief right in the workplace. But for many Cancerians, this is a welcome opportunity to help the person and the family through this rough process. Many Cancers can take it. They're well-grounded and less susceptible to the effects of feeling the negative emotions but still apt to understand them and help others navigate the choppy waters that come at the end of life. It's likely that the Cancerians who are up to this task have an earth-element moon sign, such as Virgo, Taurus, or Capricorn. Occasionally those with a fire moon-sign might also be able to rise to the occasion.

Essential Services - Electrician, Mechanic, etc.

Essential services have always been around, and only those who do the work understand the reward of a job well done. Carpenters, electricians, plumbers, and mechanics are the ones who truly understand the personal rewards of a career path where you can get your hands dirty and feel dog-tired at the end of the day.

Cancers' unexpected payoff in this type of field isn't that they can run through their energy or work mostly alone with their thoughts; it's that these services help people in ways that no one imagines until they need that support. What would happen if your refrigerator went out today? What about an air conditioner breaking down in the middle of a summer heatwave? Who do you call when your power goes out, or your car won't start? Cancers love feeling needed and helpful, and these professions tick both of those boxes.

Mechanics and electricians have the opportunity to tell people that their problem is gone, or that they can fix it. Unfortunately, they do also have to sometimes deliver the bad news that the problem requires replacement rather than repair.

What Makes Cancers Happy at Work?

Most of the time, Cancers have that strong drive toward commitment, so they want a career, not a job. Of course, the trick to finding a long-term career is to find a position or industry where you can thrive and experience happiness or contentment. Look at which Cancer characteristics are most present in your personality and use them to help you think out different career options.

These traits and the list provided here are only a starting point. Look at the career options that interest you and identify whether your personality is suited for a long-term career in that field. There are often countless ways that you can use your key characteristics, and it's evident from the high volume of Cancerian entertainers that being an extrovert or outgoing person isn't a requirement to fit into careers that initially seem out of the realm of a Cancer.

Chapter 10: Cancers On Their Own

Cancers not only love their time alone; they thrive in it. If you're a Cancer feeling overwhelmed, lost, listless, or just a little down, then take a day to yourself. Cancers don't need another person to be happy, and they are perfectly capable of making their own fun. Although they're emotional and have a deep connection to their family, they'd rather be alone if they don't have a partner. If they don't have a great family situation, they'll make their own, and it might take time, but usually, Cancers don't mind.

Not all Cancerians are introverts, and there are a few differences that come with cusp-born Cancers and between genders. There's an overarching element of comfort in solitude, though. Nearly all Cancers will need time to themselves to process their emotions, recharge, and prepare to face the next hurdle in front of them.

Cancers Need Alone Time - Even the Extroverts

To understand the relationship that Cancers have with their inner selves and why they do so well alone, we need to briefly address the subject of extroverts and introverts. Of the Big Five personality traits, extroversion is the one that receives the most attention. Technically, there isn't any such thing as an "introvert"; those described as such are just very low on the extroversion scale, and the lower on the scale, the more energy they lose around other people. Parties, social situations, and even just going to work if you work around many people can be extremely draining if you're low on the extroversion scale.

Adopting the term "introvert" to describe anyone low on the extraversion scale, we can assume that anyone drained by gatherings is an introvert. But it doesn't quite work out that way. Cancers aren't just drained because they're around people; it's because they're feeling and sensing all of those people's emotions. Cancers don't have to be introverted to enjoy time alone; even the most outgoing of Cancers will need time to recharge.

It's easiest to see this with Cancer entertainers. Unlike Leo, Sagittarius, or even fellow water-sign Scorpio celebrities, Cancers are overly protective of their alone time and their family's privacy.

To take a quick look at how extroverted or introverted-but-charismatic Cancers stack up to other signs, here's a list of a few celebrities by sign:

- Kylie Jenner - Leo (Rather open, with private life)
- David Dobrik - Leo (Rather open, with private life)
- Chrissy Teigen - Sagittarius
- Brad Pitt - Sagittarius
- Ariana Grande - Cancer (Fairly private)
- Robin Williams - Cancer (Private)

- Tom Hanks – Cancer (Private)
- Michael Jackson – Cancer (Private)

You might notice that there's a pretty evident pattern here. Cancers are more private, or to themselves, even though they can get in front of immense crowds and spend most of their time entertaining. How introverted and extroverted you are can depend on your sign, but Cancers again have a unique twist on this subject. Cancers both love people and become overwhelmed by others' emotions. It is a combination of them being a water sign, ruled under the moon, and their house representing the family. They are apt at communication and they easily dial into others' emotions, but all of this is overwhelming for them. Cancers that are low in extroversion could be more susceptible to being overwhelmed by the external emotional input and need more time alone. But how do Cancers spend their alone-time?

Crafting and Exploring

Cancers don't waste the time they spend alone the way that many other signs would. They use that time to be industrious, while also bolstering the explorative elements of their personality. They're prone to picking up new hobbies, crafting, or creating in any way possible. You'll likely find a Cancer unexpectedly picking up various hobbies and dropping them just as quickly.

Many Cancers will even use their downtime to connect with people in different ways, such as through large interactive online games or online communities.

But why all the crafting and exploring? This boils down to a mystery of Cancerians, and exactly why these signs can't keep their hands still is not exactly clear. We know that they're extremely industrious people, which is often attributed to the Moon's speed as it rushes around the earth. Cancers don't sit still, although they enjoy the occasional lazy morning before jumping into action for the rest of the day.

If you are a Cancer and looking for a way to get the most out of your downtime so you can recharge without lazing around all day, consider testing out a few different hobbies. You don't have to commit to one hobby, and you don't have to give weeks or months of your time to one pursuit.

Try these to boost your creativity and exploration during your alone-time:

- Pick up a few art supplies from a local shop

- Follow a YouTube video for painting, knitting, crochet, woodworking, or similar.

- Write a short story or record one on your voice memos.

- Put together a jigsaw puzzle, diorama, or scale model from a box (no stress in picking the "right" items)

- Try a new safe-but-thrilling adventure such as a flight simulator or diving into a story-led game (Role-Playing Game, or RPG).

- Read up or watch YouTube videos on a skill you want to improve or wished you had.

Now, if you are the friend, spouse, or close relation of a Cancer, you want to make sure you don't impede on this alone time. Cancers are not necessarily people that need to be told that they've done a good job. But when they explore crafting or have fun doing something new, they're trying to do this outside of the eye of judgment. They're doing it for themselves, but they can't just turn off their sensitive nature. Cancer men are less likely to be sensitive to judgment, but even they may feel a deep sting of their work receiving negative feedback.

So, if you walk into the room and say, "Wow, that's a really great miniature," their general feeling will be that they produced something, and now judgment or criticism has tainted it.

Cancers are often overly emotional, and when they're coming out of their alone-time, that part of their personality may be exacerbated. When Cancers seek alone-time, it's because they need to recharge, and if you invade that with your opinions and judgments, they don't have the opportunity to recharge, and they are pushed back into alone-time for even longer. They may appear to be using this time to put their feelings out there into the universe, but it's still a private affair.

One of the primary issues that Cancers struggle with, and everyone around them silently criticizes, is that they usually don't stick with more than one or two creative pursuits. They may have one or two hobbies that they go to for comfort. One male Cancer explains that he enjoys music, and because of that passion, he plays multiple instruments; he would even like to learn more, but he usually returns to the bass as his comfort zone and when he's performing with others. His secondary hobby is a well-known MMORPG (massive multiplayer online role-playing game) where he can explore even more crafting while following different storylines and engaging with others on the game's terms.

One female Cancer reports that she spends her alone-time writing screenplays; often these go unsubmitted, but she enjoys her time writing and will continue this hobby. As a secondary hobby, she enjoys crocheting, and often uses this hobby to make unique and handmade gifts for family members because she's confident in the quality of her work and her abilities.

Both the male and female Cancer mentioned here often stretch themselves beyond these hobbies. They've both tried painting, foil art, charcoal sketching, and many other things besides. The male Cancer tinkers with various electrical projects using spare or old parts to make new-ish items such as Frankenstein alarm clocks, motion detectors, and radios. The female Cancer often tries solo pursuits that take her outdoors, such as hiking, geocaching, and photography.

Why do Cancers do this? There are a few reasons behind their love of crafting and exploration and their ability to recharge when alone while also being rather busy.

1. The moon moves quickly through space, and as such, Cancers are happiest when they are in motion as well.

2. Born to the fourth house, Cancers are often looking for ways to cultivate elements of themselves that their family can enjoy too. This is where we see the rise of hobbies that offer entertainment, such as musical performance, photography, and producing crafted goods.

3. The moon, representing the soul and all things that rest beneath the surface, has Cancers constantly trying to understand themselves better. They want to know what it takes to make them content, happy, and rested.

Thinking Through the Past: The Good and The Bad

Cancers are extremely sentimental people, and they tend to revel in the past. They can spend hours going through family memories and attempting to preserve those memories through representations such as photo albums, slideshows, and journal entries. We wouldn't be surprised seeing a Cancer find an extremely creative way to preserve their memories and those personal moments that are extremely important to them.

But as sentimental people, Cancers can fall into a vortex of negative thinking on their own. They can spiral from one memory to another and then to another with very little effort. Cancerians, especially Cancer females and those on the Gemini-Cancer cusp, may have to work extra hard to move past this negative vortex. They should have a list of things or activities they can do for comfort and recharging to help pull them out of negative thinking.

For example, a Cancer woman or a Gemini-Cancer cusp person may have conditional statements to help them enjoy the past rather than get stuck in it:

- If I am feeling down and cannot get out of it, I will try a new independent hobby

- If I am stuck in the past and it's making me feel bad, I'll write (or voice memo) about the experiences and what I learned from them or how they made me stronger.

- If the first two steps don't work, I will call a supportive and positive friend to come by and spend time with me.

Although Cancers do need quite a bit of alone time, it's usually best to spend time with people they know are a positive force when they get stuck in this negative thinking pattern. Because of their heightened emotional sensitivity and their empathic abilities, being around someone who emits positive energy naturally can help lift up a Cancer. Cancers are recipients of outer energy, so their negative energy isn't going to affect those around them; instead, the nearby positive energy will affect the Cancer.

Male Cancers and those on the Cancer-Leo cusp need to take a different approach. It's often that this segment of Cancerians will need to embrace that time alone and really recede into themselves for self-reflection and to analyze or pick apart those negative memories.

Male Cancers are sensitive, but they work harder to keep their feelings and emotions to themselves. They wouldn't venture out into the world, try something new, or spend time with another person when they're feeling extremely vulnerable. For male Cancers, this is an easy equivalent of molting. When crabs molt, they will create or dig a cave and hide away; others will engage in ingenious scams that make them appear dead and unsavory to predators. This is exactly what a male Cancer is doing when they are facing internal turmoil. They hide away, protect themselves and their feelings, and eventually emerge with a new shell.

The Cancer-Leo cusps need uninterrupted alone-time for a different reason. Let's look again at the creatures which embody the Zodiac signs. We already discussed the crab's molting habits, but now there's the presence of the lion. Female lions sleep between fifteen and eighteen hours per day, while male lions sleep about twenty hours per day. This is a good indicator of the basis for an often-overlooked Leo element. Cancer-Leo cusps often require even more time to recharge. Leo's may not have the extremely sensitive disposition that Cancers do, but they wear out eventually, and when they do, they shouldn't be disturbed. Don't poke a sleeping lion, and don't mess with a molting crab. That's the combination you have when a Cancer-Leo cusp gets into a negative cycle of thinking or gets stuck on past events. They just need to accept what's happening, rest, recharge, and emerge when they are ready to face the future again.

Cancers Need Time By Themselves

Don't doubt the ability of a Cancer to thrive independently and build new experiences all by themselves. Cancers are the family house, and they do crave deep emotional connections to the few people they allow into their inner circle. They create families of their own, whether that's blood relations, friend circles, or even workplace families. They're often the nurturer and a subtle leader for any group, which can make it seem as though they constantly need people around to feed off that element of their personality.

That is the outward perspective, and Cancerians know that perspective is only one side of the coin. On the other side, you have their well-developed imagination and creative personality, which isn't usually the focus of a group setting. One of the reasons why Cancers love diverting into alone-time is that they have the opportunity to explore these elements of their personalities that they may keep secret from those around them. Anything that may appear as vulnerability is often reserved for alone-time, and that's one of the ways that they create these new experiences independently.

With the preference and ability to create something independently and then allow others to experience it later through social media, the internet, or even just sharing it with close friends, Cancers really excel at this approach. They're able to explore new hobbies and creative pursuits without limitations and then, when they are confident of their abilities, they can present what they've created to those they love and trust.

Cancerians do tend to hold on to the past, and if they weren't a cardinal sign, that might be of some concern. Under the cardinal mode, and as a water element, Cancers are prone to change. We even see this in their symbol, the crab. Crabs molt often, don't have one single home throughout their lives, and live in an ever-changing environment. Many Cancers particularly struggle with this tug-of-war between holding onto the past and moving into the future. A Cancer can learn how to balance between using the past, understanding themselves, and then creating new experiences to strengthen themselves. Then they can really thrive in almost any environment. It's the idea of using the past to create sustainable change into the future that they struggle with throughout their first few seasons in life.

During childhood and their teenage years, this particular issue will arise often, but as they get deeper into adulthood, they're able to grab hold of the new experiences they crave and use the past to direct their future. The key to achieving all of this is to develop that balance through alone-time, and the Cancer allowing themselves to spend time within their shell in order to understand themselves better.

Chapter 11: Cancers in Friendships

One of the best astrological blessings anyone could ask for is having a Cancer close to them in life. Very few signs don't mix well with Cancers (the most notable being Libras). But even Libras can often benefit from the overwhelming warmth, kindness, and generosity that comes with having a Cancer in your life. If you are a Cancer, then you should be proud of how you lift others up and bring out the best in the people around you.

It often seems like Cancers make a lifestyle out of taking care of the surrounding people. They're usually the best listeners in the group, are quick to jump in when someone needs help, and are extremely generous on a daily basis. But this often makes Cancerians constantly moody because of how much they give to the surrounding people. If you're born into the house of Cancer, then you should have higher expectations of the people around you. The one exception to this is the people born within the Leo-Cancer cusp range in which the Leo tendency to have high expectations may have nullified this issue.

If you know a Cancer and have a parent or a romantic relationship, then you should take extra care to consider their feelings and energy level. Be observant, and this chapter should have a heavy impact on you with lots of advice on what you can do to be more considerate of the Cancer in your life. As a Cancer, you should use this chapter to help you understand what to expect from others in your life.

Cancers as Friends

It's no surprise that Cancers are outstanding, once-in-a-lifetime type friends. They're family people, but to them, the family goes beyond blood. They're also extremely protective, which often means that they jump in to defend their friend when a disagreement breaks out.

If you're a friend of a Cancer, then you already know that they're always there for you and they always have your back. But you might also know that you're generally the one who also feels the pain when they're having a hard day.

Cancers love spending time with their friends in their domain, though don't be surprised if you're often the one inviting people over rather than going to a friend's house. They're also the ones to host a party, which is fairly surprising when you consider how often Cancers are more inclined toward introversion. Cancerians thrive around people that are in high spirits and, at the same time, love having a few close friends together. You can also count on Cancers to either make tasty food or arrange for the best in town.

Cancers are the "helper" friend. They listen, and their creativity from their connection to the moon and ocean makes them excellent problem solvers. Cancers generally love helping their friends smooth over any issues in their life, but they can go for long stretches of time pulled into themselves for self-reflection or to recharge.

There is a stark difference between male and female Cancers when it comes to friendships. How they make them, how many they have, and how they interact don't starkly contrast, but they go about the friendship process in different ways. Take Carrie Bradshaw of Sex in the City, a Cancer if there ever was one. She's passionate, creative, and deeply in touch with her emotions. She has three good friendships, and everyone else is really a passerby. But these friendships mean the world to her. When she's fought with friends, it has often led to many other areas of her life falling apart, which is exactly what happens in a female Cancer situation. Her friends are also predictable.

It's not just that they fit standard female HBO series tropes, but that they make sense for Carrie; she's attracted to people who communicate in mildly different ways, share similar interests, applaud her work, and have different personalities.

Male Cancers use a different approach. They're extremely self-protective, and it's usually hard to find a fictional male Cancer character because they're so hard to understand, especially in their approach to friendships. A few of the most prominent and accurately depicted male Cancerians include Walter White, Deadpool, Ron Swanson, and Peter Parker/Spiderman. What do these guys have in common? They don't really have friends. None of them. Why? Well, some of them don't have friends because they've undergone extremely traumatic events in their life and have lost loved ones, which make them afraid to make themselves vulnerable again. But Spiderman and Deadpool aside, the other two just aren't very friendly. On the surface, Ron Swanson is about as welcoming as a cactus, and Walter White wasn't much better, maybe as inviting as a shaved cactus.

But both of these characters played out a key trait among Cancers. They protected their family and the few friends they'd collected with everything they had. Walter had a few exceptions, but even in a few disputable key points, he felt as though he was doing the "right" thing for his loved one. Ron Swanson surprised viewers again and again with thoughtful but small actions of friendship, all the while putting up his strong front. This is exactly what you should expect on the surface level from a Cancer guy friend. But what about the deeper level? That's family. You can't just be a male Cancer's friend; you end up being part of the family for as long as you're willing to stick around.

Let Them Have Their Space - Physically and Mentally

Want to know how to irritate a Cancer into a week of the silent treatment? Ask, "What are you thinking about?" once too often. Depending on your Cancer friend, once more might be once too often.

How do you know when they just want alone time, and when they're more quiet than usual because something is bothering them? Anyone can answer this question correctly with one big shrug. The truth is that you'll only know based on your experience in that relationship. Cancers have an ebb and flow when it comes to their emotions, much like the tides being set in motion by the moon.

Cancers dedicate as much time and energy as possible to listening and helping others. So, when they want alone-time, they're really not asking for that much. They simply want to be left alone for a few hours, or a day, or two. But for anyone who's not a Cancer, this can be complicated to navigate. When Cancers are upset, they become quiet and often withdraw or become passive-aggressive. When Cancers need time to process the day, they withdraw and become extremely quiet. They may not want to talk about what's on their mind. In fact, the Cancer in your life probably just wants to be left alone in a room undisturbed.

It's very likely that the Cancer you know has a pet project or a variety of hobbies they want to explore and spend time working on, but they don't want other people involved. So what can you do? The best advice is to give them their space. If this person suddenly becomes quiet, don't take it as a personal offense. Don't take it as if they're giving you the silent treatment, and don't feel like you should jump up and do something. Often the best solution with Cancers is to let them take the lead. This is not like dealing with a fire sign that will blow up in a catastrophic outlash if they feel like they're not in control; Cancers are water signs, and they're usually not so over-the-top. When a Cancer wants peace, give it to them and know that they'll come around either completely fine or have a bone to pick in a calm, premeditated manner.

For Cancers, understanding your feelings and having a productive conversation after you've had a chance to think about the situation is key to keeping your beloved relationships. Many times, a Cancer is quiet, and they're not mad; they're just overwhelmed and need time to rest. This most often happens when Mercury is in retrograde or when Mercury enters Cancer. The ties between emotion and communication are always worn thin, but when they react in a way that aggravated the bond, it often means that the Cancer will shut down temporarily. That shut down is like performing maintenance or processing time. They need to recharge, and many Cancers innately know that if they try to communicate during these times that it could spell disaster.

A Cancer Will Always Communicate Their Emotions - Learn to Listen

We've spent many chapters looking at the various ways that Cancers present themselves and how they interact with people. It's easy to say that they put on a strong face, that hard outer shell, but that they're really a big softy on the inside. But that's the surface view of it. Cancers are in tune with everyone else's emotions, and they often suffer because others who aren't Cancers just can't understand them. But with practice, maybe years of practice, it is possible to understand how a Cancer communicates their emotions.

One of the most common myths or inconsistencies within modern astrological reporting is how Cancers wear their hearts on their sleeves. This couldn't be further from the truth. If you're an earth or fire sign who just isn't so receptive to Cancerian energy, or even an air sign, you might be too easily distracted to pick up on these tiny glitches in their behavior.

Let's look at one Scorpio and Cancer couple who've gone to professional counseling for their marriage. Now, the Cancer female will often put up the front that everything is fine. But it isn't fine, and the more communicative Scorpio knows that, and constantly asks the Cancer what is wrong and what he can do. That's not effective, clearly, but he doesn't understand whether she just wants alone-time, or if she's overwhelmed, or if something else is wrong.

Over many years, with the help of marriage counseling, the Scorpio has come to learn that when his wife is knitting, there's no reason to bother her. But, when she's doing domestic tasks that she often hates, such as dishes or ironing, that's the time to worry. He's also learned that when she spends time with friends, it's not because she wants distance; it's because she needs a different kind of attention, and he's put his Scorpio jealousy to the side. He takes these little cues so that he can understand what's going on in her mind. He has stopped pestering her about what she's thinking about and why she gets quiet from time to time.

Cancers are always communicating their needs and desires; it's on the other person in their life to pick up on that. This seems extremely unfair, and in many relationships or friendships, it is. Cancers that are having a tough time, or are outright depressed, can be extremely manipulative with other people's feelings. Be extremely careful in certain times of planetary movement concerning the planet Venus, as it can lead to romantic troubles, and when Venus is in Cancer, or the Moon is in Taurus, there can be great times or absolutely dire times. These changes can rock Cancers dramatically and cause unpredictable extremes. If you have a Cancer in your life, just be careful to understand their tiny hints that they're putting out into the world, hoping that someone picks upon them.

If you're the friend, spouse, parent, or child of a Cancer, there's a bit of relief ahead. The good news is that once you discover these little quirks and determine how to navigate them, you can make tremendous leaps in your relationship, whether it's romantic or otherwise.

Cancer Friendship Compatibility

Just like romantic relationships, friendships come with varying degrees of compatibility issues. The best friendship combination is a Cancer and Cancer friendship; these two truly get each other, but sometimes they can be a little too similar and get on each other's nerves, especially when they're both being moody. The next best option is for female Cancer and male Pisces, and the bond can become so deep that it almost feels psychic. The two can have deep conversations but really aren't meant for a romantic relationship. Pisces can inherently understand and respect Cancer's need for alone time. But, when it comes to male Cancers, they typically tend to prefer time around earth and fire signs. Male Cancers may find the best of friends in a Taurus, or even an Aries. For male Cancers, it's the differences that make the friendship; they want someone who is almost the opposite of what they are, to expand their world.

- Aries – Generally, for males a great friend; for women or Cancer-Leo cusps, too much to handle.

- Taurus – Great friends all around

- Gemini – Gemini-Cancer cusps know this is a friendship made in heaven, but other Cancers could take it or leave it.

- Leo – Cancer-Leo cusps know to stay away from their own kind, but pure Caners know that a Lion can bring in a ton of fun and get them out of a negative funk.

- Virgo – A grounding friend that will appreciate a Cancer the way they deserve.

- Libra – Too similar to make great friends, but good for the occasional brunch date or concert outing.

• Scorpio – Hot stuff here; a Cancer and Scorpio can make best friends for life!

• Sagittarius – This earth sign is a little too crazy and a little too self-interested to give a Cancer proper attention when they need it. Not a friendship meant to last.

• Capricorn – Great friends here, and they are often outstanding at helping each other get through hard times.

• Aquarius – Possibly the worst friend combination for a Cancer; unless you share many interests with an Aquarius, you're likely to fight constantly.

• Pisces – A friendship for the ages, although you can both bring out an unexpected competitive edge in each other. Watch out for mothering tendencies!

There are many elements that go into making a friendship compatible, and the most important one is the ability to communicate effectively. Special notes here on Aquarius and Sagittarius; these are not the best options for Cancers because of communication difficulties. An Aquarius is apt to under-communicate, and they care much more about logic and reason than feelings and fairness. Meanwhile, the Sagittarius is likely to over-communicate and overwhelm the Cancer with trivial day-to-day problems and powerful emotional frequencies.

What Cancers Wish Others Knew About Being Their Friend

In the chapter on childhood, we mentioned that Cancerians make fast friends when they're young, and then as they're older, they begin to put up a bit of a wall. So, adult Cancers will frequently turn down invitations; sometimes it's because they're genuinely busy, sometimes they're not up to the task of being around so many people, and sometimes they just don't want to do it. They may also have regular plans or routines that they refuse to break for any reason. Here are a few of the top things that Cancerians wish other people knew about being their friend.

- When a Cancer doesn't accept an invitation, don't stop inviting them.

- Go with the spontaneous ideas; they're guaranteed fun.

- Don't ask Cancers to do boring things that don't allow for conversation, such as watching a movie.

- Expect a balance of leisure and activity, although it's completely unpredictable.

Overall, Cancers are excellent friends, but they can seem like a lot of work. They're worth all of it, as they are the best listeners, among the most loyal, and without a doubt, fun.

Chapter 12: What Does a Cancer Need to Thrive?

Cancers are not as simple as they seem, but there are a few tried-and-true ways to help a Cancer thrive. There's so much available in the way of personal development that it might seem daunting even to approach the subject, much less to consider taking action. Wouldn't it be easier just to let things be? Not really. To thrive, you need to manage your weaknesses, play to your strengths, and satisfy various elements of your personality.

Cancerians might have troubles confronting their past, or for that matter, confronting much of anything or anyone at all. They might so often support others so much that they miss out. There are many times that people born under the Cancer sign give too much of themselves to others. To thrive, they need to implement a few ways to handle their day-to-day life. With routinely expanding their horizons, it's possible for Cancers to thrive in almost every situation, even when they're sensitive or feeling a bit more emotional than usual.

Work Hard, Play Hard, Rest Often

The Moon is constantly working to reflect light and brighten the night, and Cancerians often find themselves doing the same. They strive to bring light into everyone else's life, and to ensure that they're managing their needs as well as the needs of others, and take advantage of the opportunity to rest, they have to plan accordingly.

Cancer-born people play hard. Of course, that may not mean that they're out bungee jumping, going to raves, or thrill-seeking. To them, creating and exploring their natural curiosity is play. They can spend hours exploring a new hobby that they may drop the next day. Cancers tend to pick up and drop hobbies very quickly, although they likely keep one or two hobbies throughout their life. These people won't need constant reminders to practice musical instruments, put in time at the easel, or go out and snap photographs regularly. The hobbies that Cancerians pick up and keep throughout life are likely part of their regular schedule. One example of a male Cancer hobbyist photographer is proof of how far a Cancer person will go to dedicate time to play. This particular male Cancer does photography on the side, and, at pretty low rates, he offers wedding photography, pregnancy photography, and family photos. He has every weekend booked out for months, which means that he doesn't spend those weekends enjoying time with friends or relaxing at home alone. This is his version of play, and it brings him great joy. Most Cancerians have something to this effect going on in their life.

Another example is a Cancer-Leo cusp who enjoys music. This person uses a different approach to listening and engaging with music; instead of just letting the radio play, she's very intentional with her musical habits. She listens through albums from start to finish and avoids things like iTunes and Spotify. Her curious nature, which comes from Cancer, has paired with the more traditional elements that spawn from the fixed sign Leo. She listens to about two-and-a-half hours of music each day, and all of it is done with purpose.

Now, it's easy to see how Cancerians play hard, and they enjoy it. But they also work hard, and they tend not to enjoy that so much. Those born under the Cancer sign are more likely to seek out a career that actually resonates with them. It might tie into one of their many hobbies or fit directly into their high receptivity to other people's emotions. Many within the Cancer sign serve other people in one way or another through careers such as nursing, teaching, homemaking, and service industries. Even when Cancers have this outstanding degree of reward coming to them on a daily basis, they often overwork themselves. They're the ones who feel absolutely drained by the time they finally get a day off.

That degree of feeling drained brings us to the next element of Cancer in life: resting often. Not all Cancerians are introverts. But you'll often see that if there is an extroverted Cancer, they're likely in the cusp of either Gemini or Leo. Male Cancerians are more likely to be hard introverts, while female Cancerians tend to open up their friend circle a little more than the males do.

All the same, every Cancer needs time away from others, to rest and recharge so that they have complete control over the scope of emotions in their environment. They must schedule and plan out having this alone-time because they get extremely moody and passive-aggressive without it. It's not unusual for a Cancer, if they go a little too long without getting this opportunity to recharge, to lash out against those that are closest to them. If you're a Cancer, you should plan the times you're going to have to yourself. You might do this when you know that others are going to be out of the house, or specifically wake up early or stay up late to have this time alone. If you know a Cancer in your life, then make sure that you're giving them a certain degree of courtesy when they start to become reclusive.

Move Sideways Through Life

When asked how you met your Cancer friend, or when asking a Cancer how they met any of their friends, you're in for an interesting story. The famous sideways scuttle of the crab is present in everyday

Cancer interactions. They rarely enter someone's life in a straightforward method; instead, they scuttle into place.

One great example is of one of the male Cancers we've cited throughout this book. He met his romantic partner through his brother, who was dating a woman who was friends with the person who would become his wife. This is the type of Sideways Shuffle that Cancerians have in their relationships, romantic or otherwise. One of the other male Cancers used as an example in many of these chapters met his best friend through a mutual acquaintance that neither he nor his best friend actually likes spending time around. When they would show up to this person's gatherings out of courtesy, they found they enjoyed spending time together, and the friendship blossomed from there.

Beyond relationships, Cancers may experience this same sideways walk when it comes to their career. Those born under the Cancer sign will probably move into a career path that suits them well based on their personality elements and sheer convenience. They may have helped an elderly family member through later years in their life and realize that that caretaking came quite naturally to them. So it's no surprise when they got a job offer as a professional caretaker for another elderly patient and find themselves more or less entrenched in that field.

The sideways walk is a fun way for Cancerians to look at life, and they often use it to analyze their major milestones retrospectively. When they look back on how they met their best friend or significant other, found their dream job, and similar life moments, they can smile knowing that they didn't take a direct path at any of those turns.

Plan and Then Make a Plan B

One struggle that most Cancer-born deal with regularly is planning and organization. There's a lot of discussion from chapter one to this point about the Cardinal mode along with the presence of the water element and the Moon being the ruling planet, all resulting in constant and frequent change for Cancer-born. That means almost any plan a Cancerian makes is doomed before it even has the opportunity to go into motion.

Cancers should make a plan. In fact, the moon itself represents reaping the benefits of work already done; the moon reflects light already created by the Sun. The downside in the human realm is that you can't reap the benefits of work already done if you don't put in the work, to begin with. To accommodate this, Cancerians should make a plan, but they should also have a Plan B.

As with dominoes, one fall tends to lead to another, and Cancers will find that that is often the case with planning. When a Cancer-born person makes a plan, and subsequently a back-up plan, it's important that they don't focus too much on that original plan not working. If anything, they should learn to expect that their plans will not go exactly as intended, but that they'll reap an abundant and pleasant outcome in the end, anyway. Cancer should plan for their own peace of mind, and to understand what they should expect in the upcoming days or weeks. They should not fall apart into an emotional mess the moment that their plan doesn't work.

Record Your Memories and Give Them Rest

Because the Moon is so closely tied to the idea of an inner self, and the crab has that distinctive outer shell and soft interior, Cancers tend to lose themselves in thought, and particularly to thoughts of the past. Many Cancers have absolutely astounding memories, but they may put themselves into a negative spiral by reveling in memories that they can't change, and that are hurtful to revisit.

Without a doubt, there are always benefits to be found when reviewing old memories and retrospectively analyzing how you've moved through life (especially when you're prone to moving sideways and using unexpected methods). Cancers should take careful action to record their memories accurately. Many suggest journaling, but a lot of people, even Cancers, have trouble remembering to journal regularly.

We suggest using journaling, voice memo recording, or even a creative outlet such as photography, painting, or entertaining to help keep an accurate record of your memories. After you document your memories in one form or another, allow them to rest. Those born to the Cancer sun sign are exceptionally in touch with emotions, but they have trouble reflecting on their own emotions and assessing the energy that they're bringing to the environment because they're so receptive to everyone else's. When they give their memories a rest, they allow the surrounding environment to be peaceful.

Learn to Thrive Where You Are

Many Cancers report that they need seclusion and isolation and that their moodiness is something that others just have to accept sometimes. With careful planning, a solid routine, and a deep understanding of their strengths and weaknesses as a Cancer, the Cancer can fit right into almost any situation. They do well in social situations because they're often so well-liked and easy to get along with. They do well on their own because they're creative and don't need another person to entertain themselves or feel content.

The combination of being a water sign, being the Cardinal mode, under the Moon as the ruling planet, and represented by the great crab has led to a very strong personality type for Cancers. This comes with so many benefits it's almost impossible to understand them individually because they work together as a whole. This combination is truly unique, and few other signs have such a consistent presence between their element, mode, ruling planet, and symbol. They are the purest of the water signs, open to change, and ruled under the planet that symbolizes inner self, change, and emotion. Without a doubt, a Cancer is very understanding, compassionate, and caring. It is up to them to understand exactly how they can use their strengths in their everyday lives and how they can overcome a few of their weaknesses. Through the aspects of life discussed in this book, particularly those in the chapters on strengths and weaknesses, a Cancerian, even one exceptionally moody, overwhelmed, and a bit crabby, can learn to thrive.

Conclusion

Now that you are well armed with some in-depth knowledge of Cancerians, we hope you can apply this information to your daily life. Sometimes we forget to look back on the past stories that had some dramatic impact upon our world. The story of the crab who took on Heracles is a symbol today for what people can truly do, and Cancer's spot in the heavens shows that in strength and understanding, there is just reward. Cancerians often find themselves sympathetic and moved by other people's actions. But other key Cancer traits, such as an inquisitive nature or a protective tendency, may shine within your particular personality.

Use the information here to guide you through daily actions and decisions. A Cancerian is often a key decision-maker, even if they don't know it. One of their absolute strengths is a mirrored weakness: they aren't fully aware of their impact on those around them. We hope that you can assess your strengths, navigate through your weaknesses, and look to the future with hope and confidence.

Be sure to continue to track the planets and stars, and survey how those changes in the universe impact your life. Building awareness and continuing the use of astrology is often as rewarding as it is fun.

Here's another book by Mari Silva that you might like

Your Free Gift (only available for a limited time)

Thanks for getting this book! If you want to learn more about various spirituality topics, then join Mari Silva's community and get a free guided meditation MP3 for awakening your third eye. This guided meditation mp3 is designed to open and strengthen ones third eye so you can experience a higher state of consciousness. Simply visit the link below the image to get started.

https://spiritualityspot.com/meditation

References

Astrologer, M. H. M. H. and Reader, T., & Hall, author of "Astrology: A. C. I. G. to the Z. " our editorial process M. (n.d.). *The Meaning of the Cardinal Signs in Astrology.* LiveAbout. Retrieved from https://www.liveabout.com/cardinal-signs-aries-cancer-libra-capricorn-206724

Astrology.com - Horoscopes, Tarot, Psychic Readings. (2019). Astrology.com. https://www.astrology.com/

Cafe Astrology .com. (n.d.). Cafeastrology.com. Retrieved from https://cafeastrology.com

Cancer Horoscope: Cancer Zodiac Sign Dates Compatibility, Traits, and Characteristics. (2019). Astrology-Zodiac-Signs.com.

Cancer in Astrology. (n.d.). Www.Astrograph.com.

Definition of EMPATHY. (2009). Merriam-Webster.com.

webster.com/dictionary/empathy

Empathy Definition | What Is Empathy. (2009). Greater Good.

https://greatergood.berkeley.edu/topic/empathy/definition

Hermit Crab Successful Molting. (n.d.). Www.Hermitcrabpatch.com.

https://www.hermitcrabpatch.com/Hermit-Crab-Successful-Molting-a/138.htm#:

History.com Editors. (2018, August 21). *Summer Solstice.* HISTORY.

https://www.history.com/topics/natural-disasters-and-environment/history-of-summer-solstice *https://Cancerhoroscope.in/.* (n.d.). Retrieved https://Cancerhoroscope.in/ July 2017, K. A. Z. 15. (n.d.). *Cancer Constellation: Facts About the Crab.* Space.com.

Famous Birthdays. (2012). Famousbirthdays.com. https://www.famousbirthdays.com/astrology/

Majority of young adults think astrology is a science. (n.d.). UPI. https://www.upi.com/Science_News/2014/02/11/Majority-of-young-adults-think-astrology-is-a-science/5201392135954/

Mercury Retrograde Effects by Zodiac Sign. (n.d.). Horoscope.com. Retrieved from https://www.horoscope.com/mercury-retrograde/astrology/

Moon in Cancer: Characteristics and Personality Traits. (n.d.). Stars Like You. Retrieved from https://www.starslikeyou.com.au/your-astrology-profile/moon-in-Cancer/

Planetary Update by Horoscope.com. (n.d.). Www.Horoscope.com. https://www.horoscope.com

The Editors of Encyclopedia Britannica. (2018). Hera | Facts & Myths. In *Encyclopedia Britannica.*

https://www.britannica.com/topic/Hera

The Elements of Astrology: Fire, Earth, Air & Water Signs. (2016). Astrostyle: Astrology and Daily, Weekly, Monthly Horoscopes by The AstroTwins. https://astrostyle.com/learn-astrology/the-elements-fire-earth-air-and-water-signs/

Waxman, O. B. (2018, June 21). *Where Do Zodiac Signs Come From? Here's the True History Behind Your Horoscope.* Time; Time. https://time.com/5315377/are-Zodiac-signs-real-astrology-history/

What Does Your Sun, Moon, and Rising Sign Really Mean? (n.d.). Mindbody. https://explore.mindbodyonline.com/blog/wellness/what-does-your-sun-moon-and-rising-sign-really-mean

What Is Compassion? Understanding The Meaning of Compassion. (n.d.). Www.compassion.com. https://www.compassion.com/child-development/meaning-of-compassion/

Zodiac Colors And Their Meanings. (2015, March 5). Color-Meanings.com. https://www.color-meanings.com/Zodiac-colors-and-their-meanings/

CPSIA information can be obtained
at www.ICGtesting.com
Printed in the USA
BVHW061121021221
623077BV00003B/307

9 781954 029590